MIGUEL MALDONADO
LIFE LEAKAGES

First edition. June 2022
© 2020, Miguel Maldonado
📘 📷 @miguelmaldonado.oficial
✉ fugasdevida@gmail.com

ISBN: 979-8-218-01914-3
Printed in USA.

Cover design and layout: Verónica Leal
English edition and layout: Aurora Carranza

Photograph by the author

No part of this publication may be reproduced in whole or in part without the authorization of the copyright holder.

TABLE OF CONTENTS

DEDICATION AND ACKNOWLEDGEMENTS	9
INTRODUCTION	11
LIFE AND LIBERTY	15
FREEDOM AS A CONCEPT	25
LIVING SOMEONE ELSE'S LIFE MAKES US UNCONSCIOUS	33
3.1 The time we really live in.	35
3.2 The time we sell to our work.	37
3.3 Don't negotiate your authority, assume your leadership	42
OBJECTS THAT SILENTLY STEAL YOUR LIFE	45
DISTRACTION	55
YOU HAVE THE CAPACITY TO ACHIEVE ANYTHING	63
6.1 You have what you need	64
APPEARANCE	69
7.1 Change is often painful, but worth it	71
7.2 A few recommendations	74
7.3 About the job	76
TIME-WASTING ACTIVITIES	79
8.1. Enemies that damage your destiny	81
8.2 Fear	83
SECURITY DOES NOT EXIST	87
9.1 What people will say	90
9.2 In personal areas	92
MURDERED FOR FEAR OF WHAT THEY WILL SAY	95
10.1 Let go of your past	98
POSITIVE THOUGHTS	101
WE ARE ALL BORN WITH A MISSION IN LIFE	109
12.1 Deepening negative thoughts	112
BAD HABITS	119
13.1 The time of life is like a bank account	121
13.2 Toxic relationships	122

13.3 The relationship in marriage	123
MARRIAGE AND ITS CONCEPT	127
SEBASTIAN'S STORY	133
15.1 Second attempt	142
DON'T LET THE OUTSIDE COME INSIDE YOU	159
FINAL ACKNOWLEDGMENTS	163

DEDICATION AND ACKNOWLEDGEMENTS

First of all, I want to dedicate this book to my Lord, Jesus Christ, who claimed to be the way, the truth, and the life. He was my best support to be able to write this beautiful book that will undoubtedly help many people who have come to believe that there is no longer a solution to the problems they are facing.

I also want to thank my beautiful wife, Jazmín, for her unconditional support with which she has always helped me.

To my four children: Mike, Aby, Liz and Jasmine. For their love and participation in this book.

To my parents and my brothers by blood, my brothers in faith and great friends, who helped me and always encouraged me in the process of this work. To all of them, thank you so much for all the support and affection that you have unconditionally given me.

LIFE LEAKAGES

INTRODUCTION

Although sometimes life can seem very difficult and full of problems, we cannot deny that it is a privilege to be alive. Thus, life is a gift we never asked for, but was granted to us by divine will. That's why it is important to feel that we are alive. Just as when we were children and learned to eat and walk, we must learn to live without having to depend on someone else for our life to be mostly good.

In one of his famous speeches, Martin Luther King said "We've learned to fly the air like birds, we've learned to swim the seas like fish and yet we haven't learned to walk the Earth as brothers and sisters."

Although this phrase was said with the intention of ending the racial feelings of the people of that time, we can also say that we have learned to work, to use technology, to create small and big enterprises, to live inside a social system, but we have not learned to live our own lives.

As an example, let us make awareness of only three groups of people who may be trapped in a type of slavery that does not allow them to live their own lives as they would like to.

    1.   Those in a spousal relationship: their life may be slipping away from them and they do not perceive it because they are too busy taking care of their partner's life, everything they do is not for

themselves, but for the benefit of the other. And although this is something that may sound very nice and romantic, truth is that it's not because, in most cases, these people depend on their spouse to be good or kind or grateful for them to be happy, but if they are not, then happiness will not come. That is why many people think they will be happy when their partner changes their attitude, but no one can change anyone and you can be happy and live your life without expecting for someone to decide to make a change for your benefit.

2. People who work: Due to the social system in which we live, we are forced to work to obtain the economic resources to live. The problem with this is that we often do not realize that most of our years are invested in a job that we do not like. We live with the hope that someday retirement will come, and that it will be then when we can begin living our lives. In the meantime, we are wasting our time because we ignore that, although working is necessary, living our lives is an urgency. Therefore, if work is not good enough for us to like and enjoy, we should know that there are thousands of ways to earn a living so that we can enjoy work and life at the same time.

3. Entrepreneurs: For a long time there has been a misconception of what it means to be successful. It has been said that to achieve your goals, you have to put your life on hold and start suffering, because success takes a lot of hard work and often takes you away from the people you

LIFE LEAKAGES

love. To believe in this misconception is terrible because a person starts to sacrifice oneself by working more than recommended, he stops eating the dishes he enjoys supposedly to be able to save money, he starts to be absent from home, supposedly to provide his children a better life, and he has no break from work, even if he is sick or weak, he must continue to work hard in the hopes of benefitting from all that sacrifice. But think that your life is more important than anything else. You cannot put it on hold, but you have to learn to enjoy the process of the path toward your goals and learn to live while you succeed, because it is a fool's errand to stop living to start succeeding. Times have changed and today I am sure you can do both: live and achieve success at the same time.

Surely you have heard the saying you only live once. This way of thinking is fatal and wrong because the truth is quite the opposite, we only die once but we live every day. From the morning when we open our eyes, we have a new opportunity to live, or just exist.

Because living and existing are different. For example, airplanes exist, cell phones exist, televisions, cars, businesses, among many other things, exist, but all of them only exist and do not live. You have to ensure that you are living because it is not enough just to exist and be part of a system or to be a number more in government records. You are here to live and enjoy life until the last breath and be able to leave a very good legacy for your future generations.

Since I was a child, I began observing how people struggled to survive and how the pressure of this society leads you to imitate others, making you forget to live your own life. As a minister and counselor, I have talked with many people who at some point lost the sense of being alive and are just existing. I have observed firsthand how tragic it can be for a person to stop living before going to the grave. That is why I wrote this book, to send a message to you, whoever you are and wherever you are, to help you realize that you are alive, that you are not a work machine or a puppet that others can use to benefit themselves, and that, even if you are sharing your life with someone, you belong to no one. I want to tell you before it is too late that you have a life of your own that God gave you and that you have to take advantage of the fact that you still have time left to stop existing and start living.

    I am fully convinced that this book will be a tool that God will use to start the engines of your life so that you can live with the enthusiasm you need as you go through this beautiful, yet aggressive world. And I promise you that when you finish reading this book, your life will never be the same again.

LIFE LEAKAGES

Chapter 1
LIFE AND LIBERTY

*"The time we enjoy in the company of others
is the time that is actually lived."*

Life is a winding road full of situations that will test us. It is up to us to choose the path in which we want to travel it or wait until the last minute of our time on this world to go out there and do something worthwhile.

As Patrick Henry once said in his famous speech during the fight for the independence of the United States: "Give me liberty or give me death." This expression had such an impact on society that it led thousands of people to realize that it was useless being alive without being *free*. And just as in life, there are thousands of traps that at first glance look beautiful, but later turn into pitfalls from which it is almost impossible to get out, unless you decide to fight with your own life to be free again.

One of the things I do as a minister is visiting people in prison and, on many occasions, I can see the same expression in some who are serving their sentence. I often hear laments of extreme hopelessness from inmates who suffer from the fact of being incarcerated and not being able to continue with their lives in a normal way, according to them as when they were free.

That is why I want to take this moment to share with you something that I learned during these prison visits as a chaplain. Many times, when I start talking to these people, I ask them: If, for some reason, you could be released right now, what would you do if you were free? I almost always get *the same answer.*

In a very desperate yet excited way, I hear them say: "I would run to hug my spouse, hug and kiss my children, apologize to the people I have offended, start the business I always wanted or become a successful businessman."

But then they look down and go on saying: "But I'm a prisoner in this place, my life is passing by and I'm missing the best of it." To hear them talk that way, it might seem that it is the bars that prevent them from realizing their desires or goals.

I want you to pay attention to what I will tell you next: When I ask them the following questions is when they realize that their life is being wasted. Even before they went to jail, they were already prisoners of a culture, tradition, or habits.

The questions are as follows:

» "Did you use to embrace your spouse the way you would embrace them now?" The answer is No.

» "Did you use to hug and kiss your children as you would hug and kiss them now?" Answer? No.

» "Were you previously able to apologize to the people you offended?" Guess the answer! Exactly, it's a no.

» "Did you use to have that same enthusiasm and did everything that could lead you to start the business or the company you want? I mean, were you studying things about your future business? Were you attending conferences? Were you buying

LIFE LEAKAGES

and reading books that would make you a better entrepreneur?" The answer? A big, sad NO.

You see? These people were already in prison, their life no longer had a direction or a successful destiny. Now you may be asking yourself: "But, were they imprisoned? For what reason? And, in what way?"

Well, to understand fully, let's first take a look at the beginning of all things. I don't know if you believe what the Bible says, but let's take its texts as a reference to understand the present state of these people who were already in mental prisons, which drains the life out of human beings.

According to the Bible, in the first chapter of Genesis, it is mentioned that before the man was created, the Creator made everything that exists. That is, everything that human beings would need to live was made first, meaning that everything was done without anything missing, every detail in the universe, as well in the Earth, was created in a perfect way to serve human beings.

So only when everything was done did the Creator make the man.

I also want you to notice something very important here. The Man was created to enjoy what was made by God and to reign over the created things; that is, humans were created and designed to be the boss of things and not to be a slave of them. Almost always, to feel secure, we like to be in control of everything and we like working positions where we can exercise domination because that is what we were made for. In other words, I want to tell you that when you were created, first you were born in the thoughts of God.

The Bible says in Jeremiah 1:5, "Before I formed you in the womb I knew you."

This means that before you came into this world, you had an encounter and a conversation with God, and during that conversation, you were the person that, inside yourself, you want to be now. From before *you* were born it was decreed that you would be born to have power over the circumstances you might face and not for them to control you.

Also, everything that exists was made for you, so that you would not lack anything. If right now you do not feel complete and you are not happy because you think something is missing, then I can assure you that it is because you were not born to be limited or to be crushed by the problems that may be attacking you.

Returning to the subject, the human being was created to be free and to lead, but a person who is imprisoned, who is not free, cannot be a leader of anything. In fact, whoever is behind bars does not even have the rights of someone that is free.

So, we can say that you need to know the purpose for which you came to this earth so you can fulfill it, to have the certainty that many things in this world rightfully belong to you, but if you are trapped in a mental prison you will not be able to obtain them.

These barriers can be thoughts such as, I have no money, I can never do anything right, I come from a dysfunctional family, I have no education, I have no job, I am very ugly, I got divorced, among others.

Culture and society have made us believe that we are worth according to what we have, that's why we fall for and believe in these lies. They become prisons in our minds, and just as someone who is behind bars and has lost everything would say something like: "I would be so happy if I could be near my loved ones," so do many others as well. They don't realize of what they have until they lose it.

In the same way, we can hear other people who are surrounded by their loved ones saying: "I would be so happy if I could buy that house," or that car or that brand of clothing or anything else.

But why do we have to wait for something to happen to be happy?

Most people wait for a certain phase of their life to think about happiness. We say things like:

» I'm going to be happy when I graduate from college.

» I'll be happy when I become independent from the house of my parents and I go to live alone.

» Happiness will find me when I have a partner.

» The day I get married, I will be the luckiest person in the world.

» When my children are born, I will be filled with euphoria.

» If I manage to buy my first car, I will be the luckiest guy in the neighborhood.

» As soon as I have my own business, I will have everything.

» If I live long enough to meet my grandchildren, I will lack nothing in this life.

The end of our life comes, and just when we find ourselves laying in a hospital bed, delirious, almost waiting for our last breath, whether we are surrounded by our loved ones or alone -as it happens to many people who do not make the right decisions throughout their time on this earth- we ask ourselves: "When was it supposed to be the time to be happy?"

> •
> *Before you were born it was decreed that you were born to have power over the circumstances you might face and not for them to control you.*
> •

Our life goes by so quickly that it may be that, even lying in bed staring at the white of a hospital ceiling, at that moment when we realize that we wasted our life, that we did not enjoy every moment as if it were our last, that we did not enjoy our family or our loved ones while we still could, that we did not leave that job we never liked because there always seemed to be a compelling reason to put things off and that, at the end of our existence, it no longer seems so important.

I remember one day a friend invited me to go fishing. To be honest, I don't like to eat fish, but I really like fishing, so I immediately accepted the invitation. He told me he had found a place where there were a lot of fish. I got into his car and he drove until we came to a very small lake. It was a little smaller than half the size of a football stadium, but I was surprised that, despite being very small, there were about thirty people and each one had up to three hooks in the water, and they were all catching lots of fish.

Then I thought about how difficult and dangerous it must have been for those fish to live in such a small lake and with that many hooks that pretended to be delicious food but in reality, were deadly traps that would end their lives. Back at home, while we were listening to some music, I could perceive that life was teaching me something very important.

The teaching was that, like fish, we humans live in a very small world full of traps disguised as something

LIFE LEAKAGES

good or beautiful. For example, since the beginning of the day we hear advertisements on television, on the radio, or even see them on the way to work, school, or anywhere: advertisements that offer us their products with the goal of convincing us that *we lack something and that only they have it*. That is marketing's greatest strategy: making you believe that you can't be happy with what you have and that you need what they are offering you.

Like the fish, you can be a victim of these traps disguised as something good, but which leads you into debt. If you get into debt, you will have to work more to pay off the debt; if you work more, you will neglect your life and your family; if you neglect your family, you will end up losing their respect and in the worst case, you will end up losing them, all this by falling into one of the thousands of traps that are sold to us daily. These traps steal your time and with it your life.

As people, we come to think that a prison is terrible place, that it is a place where we never want to be; however, we have to realize before it is too late that the physical prison is only a *mirror* of what a prison looks like in the mind of an individual.

Another clear example I want to share with you is what I have learned from visiting hospitals, as I am often invited to accompany a person who is about to die. I always ask them the question: "What would you do if you had the chance to live one more year of life?"

And just like in prisons, I always hear the same response, usually, something like: "I would love more, value my spouse and family more, travel more, I would diet less, care less about what people think or say about me," among many other things.

Although there are exceptions. Some have said to me: "Well, yes I did," then close their eyes, let out some very thick tears, and continue: "But I didn't do it the way I would have liked to."

I am also sure that you have heard of someone or met someone who unfortunately, was diagnosed with a terminal illness and only has a few months or days to live. You may have noticed that, when that happens, the person who is going to die stops what they are doing and gets on with living their life. But what do they have left? The most regrettable thing is not that he has realized that he is going to die, but what torments him most is knowing that he is going to leave this planet without having lived his life, having wasted it in banal things that were not worthwhile.

In such difficult moments, the family unites and dedicates time to this person. They invite them to travel or to visit the sea. Why? Because that is when they realize that what they are going through does not make much sense and what matters most in life is that it should be lived before it ends.

Dear friend, let me tell you that your life has a clock that does not stop and every hour, minute or even second lost can be fatal if it is not taken advantage of as it should be.

That is why I encourage you to stand up, to fight for your freedom so that you can live. Remember that you were created to rule, to have dominion over your life, to be above and not below. You were born to be a hunter and not to be the prey, you were born to lend and not to borrow.

> *Show life that it doesn't matter where you came from but where you are going, that it doesn't matter how you started but how you are going to finish.*

LIFE LEAKAGES

Once again I say to you: go ahead! You were created for a purpose and the creation needs you. Try hard and draw strength from your weakness, show life that it doesn't matter where you came from but where you are going, that it doesn't matter how you started but how you are going to finish. You were born to win battles, and although you may have lost some, the war is not over yet. Get up, shake off the laziness and negative thinking. Decide to be free so that you can say as Patrick Henry said when America's independence was being fought for: "Give me liberty, or give me death!"

LIFE LEAKAGES

Chapter 2
FREEDOM AS A CONCEPT

Freedom is the gift with which we are all born, but few manage to preserve. We are in the information age. If you search the internet for the meaning of freedom you will find these two important points:

1. The faculty and right of individuals to responsibly choose their own way of acting within society. Freedom is a basic human right.

2. The state or condition of a free person, who is neither in prison nor subject to the will of another, nor constrained by obligation, duty, discipline, etc.

Broadly speaking, what we can learn from both statements is that freedom is something we all have since we have free will. No one can force us to do anything we do not want to do, unless it infringes on the freedom of others or the laws established for living in society.

As Jean-Paul Sartre famously said, "My freedom ends where the freedom of others begins."

Freedom is what we are born with. The first basic human right we have when we come into this world. Every human being has this privilege; however, it is important to understand that we are born into a religion or a culture, and around people who love us but in many cases deprive us of our freedom because they require us to learn the things that they think are the best. They force us to practice a religion or a belief that someone instilled in them; in fact, we are forced to think the same as the rest of the family. That is where our freedom begins to end, but something important to note is that when a human being is born into a very poor family, full of limitations and mediocrity, they still want to force him to believe, think or do things the way they are used to doing. If it has not worked for them for years and they continue to live in misery, what makes them think that continuing to believe in the same way will make any difference? After all, we know that changes come when mindsets are changed.

Although we are all born with the right to be free, over time we become accustomed to the traditions that our ancestors practiced and give up the right to think for ourselves, we give up the right to our freedom.

As we said before, human beings came into this world to live happily and enjoy everything that was already made. Remember that, although one person could not create everything that exists, we have to believe that everything that exists was created for the human race.

In the beginning, the desire of our Creator in forming us was that we should lack nothing, and in fact, according to the sacred scriptures, God himself breathed into the human being so that he could live. If this is so, we can say that in each person there is the breath of God, and do you know what this means? That there is a spirit of greatness within you that, although you cannot see it now, if you make an effort, you will reach the fullness of your destiny. You were created to live and enjoy the best of the best. However, we have to note that, although God's desire was for mankind to live in

LIFE LEAKAGES

freedom and in a place where nothing would be lacking, one day something unexpected happened. According to the Bible in the book of Genesis, one day an enemy in the form of a serpent entered that place and began to tell lies to the people who had been created to have everything.

But the moment they heard these lies and believed them, they lost the right to enjoy everything and to possess what they had been given. They had to abandon the lifestyle they had been leading, but the most terrible thing is that their happiness ended and the pain began.

As I mentioned before, I don't know if you believe in the Bible or not, but this story keeps repeating itself day after day in our lives. If you allow me, I would like to help you and for you to help me take a trip back in time. Yes, that's right! We will travel back in time when you were just a baby, is that okay? Yes? Then open your imagination and come with me.

You probably don't remember when you were one to five years old; however, you were most likely a happy child, no matter what was going on around you. Life seemed to be full of new things to discover, everything was happiness, you had someone who loved you, cared for you, and was with you, and there was no suffering or fear.

Let's continue. You are eight years old now, in here everything was pretty, you play a lot, you have fun and even though sometimes you cry, there are more times when you laugh. You don't worry about anything, you don't even realize if your clothes are from a recognized brand, if it's common or old. You just live, you are happy and you don't care if the world is at war or if it is in crisis. At the end of the day, when you go to your bed to sleep, you just remember all the things you did and you wish for day to come to run and sweat again, to feel the wind on your face, to search for new adventures. Although you listen the adults talk about money or stuff that worries them, the truth is that you don't care a bit. Do you know why? Because until this moment you are living the purpose for which you were created.

You live in a free way, you aren't trapped in fashion styles or the scams of riches. Up to this point everything you do is enjoy and everything seems easy to you. In fact, very often they called you out because, according to them, you were not taking things seriously, but what was happening was that you had a child's mind. That is, you were free and nothing seemed impossible to you.

Just to add something to this, it's important to know that one day, Jesus of Nazareth told the adults that the kingdom of heavens belongs to the children. This is because in childhood it seems to us that there is nothing impossible. We request to buy us a lot of stuff and we don't understand when we are told that it can't be done, because at that age we still have the winner's mind that God put in each one of us.

But let's go to when you were ten years old. Although you are still happy, you have encounters with that enemy that presented itself to you in the form of a snake. It comes to you in the form of a parent who mistreats you or people who tell you to behave but do just the opposite. For example, a relative told you never to drink alcoholic beverages but you see them with a bottle of wine in his hand. So, here you realize that people lie and don't do what they say. Then you also lie and try to pretend to be something you are not, and here you start to lose your authenticity; you stop being legitimate and start to live like everybody else.

LIFE LEAKAGES

Now let's take a trip to your fifteenth birthday. Here you are still having fun, but now it is different. Maybe your enemy came in a different form, so you did not recognize him and he took away your right to be happy. Maybe he came as a special person you fell in love with and gave them your trust, your heart; you thought they would never betray you. But things didn't turn out the way you expected and they broke your heart. You began to feel that agonizing jealousy, thinking of revenge and following perverse friends just to look good to others. You give up more and more of yourself and fill yourself with the expectations of others just a little bit more and more.

Let's go to your twenties. Maybe here you already have many responsibilities that you didn't have at fifteen. You have to go to work, maybe you are already married and have a relationship to develop, and maybe you already have children. Anyhow, by now you may have a life full of activities that you don't realize are imprisoning you, in places where your enemy locked you up, and the circumstances are the ones that rule your life. That is, you depend on everything being okay, so you can be okay; you depend on the circumstances being in your favor to be happy. But today you are here reading this book to know that you were not born to be a slave to the circumstances of life. You were born to be a leader, there is a spirit of greatness within you that is asking to break out of that confinement and fulfill its purpose.

I heard it said one day that there are three types of people on this planet. The first is made up of those who never know what is happening, then some always ask what is happening, and then some that make things happen.

I encourage you to become one of those who make things happen. Remember: someone who governs is someone who is free, so get out of those prisons of fears, resentments, hatreds, and all those things that do not allow you to bring out your potential to lead. When you rule your own life, you will also help others to convert, from being prisoners, to being completely free.

It is very important to note that the most famous and important man who ever walked this planet was Jesus Christ. In fact, the years of time were divided before him and after him. This man, who introduced himself as the son of God, began his ministry with the following words as related in the gospel of Luke 4:18:

"The Spirit of the Lord is upon me, because he has anointed me to preach the Gospel to the poor. He has sent me to heal the brokenhearted, to preach deliverance to the captives and recovery of sight to the blind, to set at liberty those who are oppressed, to preach the acceptable year of the Lord."

Do you see? In the beginning, God had made mankind to be happy, but when Christ comes he finds the opposite: poor, depressed, captive, and blind people mistreated by a system.

In other words, they were living the opposite of what they were created for. I don't know who you are, I don't know where you're from, I don't even know your name, but I'm sure you were born to be free and not to be trapped by poverty, depression, or the despair of some disease. If you are and you are tired of an oppressed and meaningless life, I have good news for you: there is hope for you. No matter what your present is like, I assure you that, if you decide today to be the person you were created to be, your end will be very good.

LIFE LEAKAGES

Because it doesn't matter where you came from, it doesn't matter where you are going to go, and it doesn't matter what your social status is. To make a change, only your mental and emotional state matters, and later I will show you some tools you can use to heal the wounds someone has inflicted on you so that you can move through life as a free person.

So, I encourage you to stand up and not to faint or give up, that the best times are coming for your life, the best things are yet to come.

There is a drizzle of good things that is looking for you. Just keep standing and you will see how that overcoming spirit in you will manifest itself and everyone will know that you were made for great things.

You will soon realize that you were not born to be on the ground or to live in suffering, but because this world needs you, and there is a task for you, and no one but you can do it. That is why your enemies fear you, and the way to stop you is to make you believe that you cannot do it.

That is why, since your childhood, you were marked by scarcity, so that you believed this was your destiny, but today you can get up, shed all those fears, and stand up. Show your enemies that you are still alive and that as long as you have life, you also have the hope that things will change in your favor.

You were not born to lose, but to win. You are not here to beg but to give. You did not come here to borrow, but to lend.

In you is the capacity to win, no matter what the circumstances are and although you have probably lost some battles, the war is not over. Take courage to fight for your freedom because you were born to live God's thoughtful design, and if God himself sent his son to set you free it is because he loves you, believes in you, and wants to see you free and triumphant.

In the Gospel of Matthew 18, Jesus said that if we do not become like children again, we will not be able to see the Kingdom of God.

This is because, in the kingdom of God, there are no limits, there is no poverty, sickness, hatred, or anything that can stop you. When you were a child, you lived in the Kingdom of God. Now, do you understand why nothing stopped you and nothing was impossible for you? Because you were original, authentic, and had the mentality of the Heavens. That is why it is important that we gain that mentality again because only with a kingdom mentality can we overcome the circumstances of this world.

Have you ever noticed that children can fight and get angry, but they don't hate? No matter how many times they fight with another child, after a while they will be talking or playing again.

That is why, if we want to overcome hatred and resentment, we need to be ourselves again! That is, as when we were legitimate, as when we were children!

LIFE LEAKAGES

Chapter 3
LIVING SOMEONE ELSE'S LIFE MAKES US UNCONSCIOUS

An interesting question to ask in this chapter is that if we were born to be free and to rule, how did we get to a state where we sometimes need psychological help or self-help therapies to survive?

This happens because we become unconscious. For example, when someone is asleep, we can observe them and we know for sure that they are there, but they do not know that we are there because they are unconscious and, consequently, do not realize that someone is next to them.

Now imagine that if a thief were to come along, he could steal everything but the person sleeping would still not know what is going on around them. Therefore, they won't realize that they have lost everything they had. In fact, if unfortunately, an earthquake happened at that moment, they would probably die by being hit by the materials of their house and would not be able to escape because of their unconsciousness. That's how dangerous it is to walk and live this life unconsciously.

Likewise, you may be belittling and ignoring the people around you who love you but you do not value them because you are not aware that it is a blessing to have them by your side. You may even be losing everything you love because you don't realize what you have, or you may be losing your life because you are absent and don't realize you are dying. It may sound like an exaggeration but stop and think about it for a moment. When a person is born, we think that their life is beginning; that is, we can assume that when a baby is born it is the beginning of their life, of their journey through this world. This happens because we look at a person in a very tiny body, we see them growing and the growth is a slow progress to become something bigger. But life does not progress that way, it is just the opposite. Life goes from *more to less*.

Let me illustrate this with an example from yourself: Let's say when you were born, you were given a certain amount of time that no one knows, but we do know that this time is limited and that one day it will end.

This would be similar to an hourglass with a countdown timer. If you look at it this way, I am sure you will be more aware of how to live and invest your time wisely because, although you have your hands, your feet, your eyes, and all your organs, truly the most valuable thing you possess is the time that by divine will was given to you.

Now think –that in this world, you can acquire many valuable things, *but you will never get more time* than the one assigned to you. That's why you should be aware that your life is not based nor depends on how you look on the outside, where you live, or what car you drive. Your life is based on your actions, on what you invest your time in. Remember that every minute and every second are of utmost importance to you because you can never get back the time you spent wrongly, so I invite you to be aware that you are alive, to make the most of your time. No matter where you are, where you live, or what you believe in, if you are breathing right now you still have time to redeem your life so that at the end of your days you don't lament; you can get the most of your time and, at the end of your life, you can say with great satisfaction, without regrets: "What a life I lived. I'm satisfied."

3.1 The time we really live in.

To help you get the most out of your time, let's first take a very cautious look at what most of the time in our lives is spent on.

For this, we will use as an example, the lifestyle of an average person.

According to certain statistics in the United States, a person has an average lifespan of eighty years. Now, if the eighty years that a person can live were exact, it is here where we can see how much of that time is truly lived. So, I ask you to pay close attention so that if you find something that identifies with you, you can understand it and make an urgent change in your way of living to make the most of the time you have left on this planet.

Taking into account that a person lives eighty years, we would have to subtract the first five because no matter how beautiful they may have been, during that time they are unconscious, which means I am almost sure that you do not remember anything from when you were that age and that, if you remember something, it feels more like a dream than a memory, right? So instead of eighty we only have seventy-five years to live.

All right, well, from these seventy-five years, we have to eliminate the time we are asleep because, as we said, when a person is asleep they are unconscious. They cannot make decisions and do not know what is going on around them, so it is as if they were not alive.

According to other statistics, people sleep an average of about eight hours a day. If this is true and we do the math, it equals 2,920 hours in a year, which can be counted as 121 days, or approximately 4 months. Can you imagine? Almost a third of a year is the time a person can be unconscious, that's to say, asleep.

Now let's divide the seventy-five years you are going to live by the four months we spend lying down and sleeping in bed: the result of this time equals sixteen unconscious years of your life.

To put it more clearly, this means that of the seventy-five years a person can live, sixteen years will be spent *sleeping*.

So, we can assume that instead of a person living seventy-five years, they will actually live only fifty-nine years. Unbelievable! It seems that sleeping a lot is not a very smart thing to do, is it?

Very well, if we know that we only have fifty-nine years left to live, it is going to be a very short time, so we will surely take much better care of it. But we cannot take that for granted because, although fifty-nine years is what a person can be conscious and living, we would have to look at what they spend their time on. For example, we all have to work and if you have a job, although it sounds a bit strong and exaggerated, you should know that what truly happens when we are looking for a job is that we

> Although one person may live seventy-five years, in reality they will only live fifty-nine. It seems that sleeping a lot is not a very smart thing to do, is it?

are selling our life. When we arrive at an interview our future boss decides how much to pay us because he needs us to be at his disposal, which means that during working hours you no longer have the same rights as when you are not working. When you are working you can't answer your cell phone no matter if the person who is calling you is the person that you love the most. As long as someone is paying for your time, the one who decides what you should and shouldn't do is your boss and not exactly you.

Of course, you will always have the option to quit, but that will not be the path you want to take and go on unemployment. But later in this book, I will give you some good tools that you can use so you can be free and able to decide about your own life.

3.2 The time we sell to our work.

Let's say that on average people start working at the age of eighteen. In the United States, people can retire at sixty-two, but with limited benefits. To receive their full benefits, most retire at sixty-seven. So, if a young man starts working at eighteen and retires at sixty-seven, we can say that he has worked forty-nine years.

A person works an average of fifty hours per week because most of the time they work six days, or instead of working eight hours a day, they work ten hours a day. If it is fifty hours per week, this is equivalent to two hundred hours per month and, to finish soon, if you add it you may realize that the time worked will be of almost fifteen years. Can you imagine? You have sold fifteen full years of your forty-nine conscious working years!

Not to mention that at some point in your life, you will probably work part-time somewhere else. But we will close this account in which fifteen years of our life are sold to a job from which we will obtain the economic resources to support ourselves and our family. So, of the fifty-nine years we had of conscious life, we only have forty-four free years to invest them in whatever we want.

Now, I want you to pay close attention because it may be that you are also wasting a lot of this time without realizing it, that's why I invite you to look very carefully at how we live our days.

Let's start by being fully aware and remembering how your day starts. For example, let's assume you have a job from seven in the morning to five in the afternoon. When you wake up, you are sure to have a lot of energy because you had a good night's sleep; your body is rested, and your brain is fresh. You get up and go to work.

When you arrive at work you can be very motivated because you are full of energy. You may be chatting with your colleagues, laughing, giving good ideas, and even being very productive. But when the workday is over you have used up all your energy and no matter what you do or what you have done, whether you are an employee, an entrepreneur, or a very smart business person, at the end of the day, you are likely to go home tired and frustrated.

When you leave your job or whatever it is that you do, that's when your free and conscious time begins. This is where you have the opportunity to invest the little available time you have left to build a future for yourself or leave a good legacy to those you love. Or simply, to be happy. That is why you should know that the most important time is not the time in which you feel livelier or more rested, but it is the time you have not sold out, that is, the time in which you decide what you will do. You must be careful to make good use of that free time.

I know that sometimes it is extremely difficult to be at work for long hours, and then have to come home and give the best of ourselves, but this is the most productive time you can have in the day because, at the end of the day, for your boss, you are just a number that can be replaced, but for those who love you, you are everything.

On a certain occasion, I joined a gym and started working out a bit but whenever I felt I was getting tired I would immediately stop. Then my trainer came to me and explained that there was no point in doing that kind of exercise. He told me that when I began to lift the weights nothing was hurting me and I was able to do it with ease, but after several repetitions, my muscles started to hurt and that's what was making me stop, but that it was precisely there when the exercise began to take effect; meaning that when the body begins to hurt is when the muscles are, in fact, getting stronger. Before the pain, it doesn't matter how many times you lift the weights. What truly matters is how many times you can lift them up after it begins to hurt. It's the same with your free and conscious time productivity. Going to a job is common and almost everybody does it in a natural

> *At the end of the day, to your boss, you are just a number that can be replaced, but for those who love you, you are everything.*

way, but it's only after they're tired and exhausted that you can distinguish the dreamers from the conformists, the ones who stop because of pain or fatigue from the ones who struggle even in the midst of pain and the ones who decide to do worthwhile things from those that only dedicate themselves to rest and waste their real free time. In the end, no matter what they do, rest assured that with time they will see the true results of their little or considerable effort.

You must be aware that the time you were working was a sold time that does not belong to you but to your boss, and everything you did was in exchange for money. You worked on the dreams and goals of your employer, but it's in your free and conscious time that you can work on your dreams and your goals. I encourage you to be brave and fight for what you want. Maybe all you need is to spend some time with your family and create good moments with them to leave them with a legacy of good memories so that, when you are no longer here, they can follow your example and will remember that you only left them good things.

But sadly, in most cases, when someone returns home, they go to their family with the worst version of themselves. This is because, as previously mentioned, almost always all of our energy and the best of us is given to a job or some colleagues, and in those moments the desire to smile and make people laugh is over. Then a person comes home and shows the worst to his children and spouse, and gives them their tiredness, their frustration. That is why today you will see people come home after a long day at work and demand to be left alone because they are tired and think that everyone at home should understand. But because children don't

LIFE LEAKAGES

understand, they may insist that they play with them, which can lead to increased stress and yelling without measuring the consequences.

Now you may be wondering, what does this have to do with the time in my life? How can this be a leakage of life?

The apostle Paul said: "He who does not rule his own house well will not be able to rule anything." It means that if you are not a good leader at home, you will not be a good leader outside your home either. Your family is the best place to develop your leadership and grow as a person. If you are not spending quality time with them and leaving them a good legacy now, today is a good time to realize this mistake.

Many times we think that we make enough effort at work and bring home everything that is needed so that our family lacks nothing. Although this is a very good thought, as well as a very good intention, we have to accept that many times we have used it as an excuse to live selfishly and in our own way. As in the previous example, even today we can see leaders of large companies, businesses, or religious organizations coming to their homes demanding that they be given their space because they need to be alone. This is sometimes understandable because, in business or wherever you are a leader, you are surely surrounded by many people, but it is unacceptable for someone to keep giving their best to strangers and their worst to their loved ones.

The truth is that when a person does not make good use of their free and conscious time with their family, they become selfish and demand to be understood, to be served everything at hand while they spend long hours watching their cell phone, and to be respected because they are the ones who provides for the family. But remember that you are a leader and you cannot negotiate your authority because the day will come when you can no longer work and then someone else will tell you: "Now I am the one who provides for the family, don't bother me."

3.3 Don't negotiate your authority, assume your leadership

I don't know if you are a man or a woman, but if you have children, you should know that you are a leader and that you are in that home to lead your home well. Remember that a leader is not the one who commands but the one who sets the example. The greatest leader that this planet has ever had was Jesus of Nazareth. And it was Jesus who said: "For even the Son of Man did not come to be served, but to serve."

This means that, if you do not develop in serving others, you are not an authentic leader. You may be a boss or a big shot, but your family does not need a boss, they need a leader who teaches them by example the best way to live this life.

So, if you invest your time well with the people you love and who love you, I assure you that you will be happier and more productive. Draw strength from your weaknesses so that when you get home, your family can see the arrival of the hero

Your family does not need a boss, they need a leader who teaches them by example the best way to live this life.

LIFE LEAKAGES

they need. Remove your tired expression and put a smile on your face because no matter how effective you are outside your home or if you achieve the success you have always dreamed of, in the end, the only ones who will be there for you will be your family. They are your fellow travelers through this life. Invest the best in them and this will be like a good deed in which if you sow the best, you will also reap the best. Dare to live the true leadership that was designed for you and live and enjoy the most of your free and conscious time. You may not be able to avoid going to a job or having to sleep and being unconscious all that time, but what you can do is to avoid being unconscious with your family and not realizing all the damage you cause when, even though you are present, you want them to live as if you were not. But I am sure that times will change in your favor. I trust and pray to God that after you read these words, your life will be even better than it already is. I believe with all certainty that, if you finish reading this book, in the end you will no longer be the same and that without realizing it, your life will begin to transform so that you will take advantage of every second and every minute of your time that by divine will was given to you.

Keep in mind that you were created with all the capabilities to create a safe environment for you and your people.

LIFE LEAKAGES

Chapter 4
OBJECTS THAT SILENTLY STEAL YOUR LIFE

Here I want to share with you some other things that can be a life leak and, if you don't detect them in time, they will finish you off. As in prisons, leakages deprive us of our freedom and we will only be able to leave when we serve our sentence. However, as I was telling you at the beginning of this book, prisons are also the best place for a person to realize how bad it feels to have wasted one's life. So, to help you, I need you to agree with me that a prison is a place that is not so easy to get out of.

A bad habit that we cannot stop and that is controlling us can also become a prison, and a prison, as we have already assumed, is a leakage of life that can take away our treasured time.

These bad habits that take away our valuable time can be a vice to a substance or some kind of drug, but they can also be objects. These can be a cellphone, television, video games, a computer, and so on.

But now let's talk about television. This device that is nothing more than metal and plastics has the same effects as a very dangerous drug. Maybe now you think I'm crazy, but I want you to think of a person addicted to a drug as dangerous as cocaine. Intoxicated by that substance, they can be very violent, but they depend on its use to find meaning in their lives. In fact, when they are not using it, they are often violent and dangerous even to their own family, but if you talk to any of them, they will tell you that they are not addicted and that they can quit the drug whenever they want. The same can be said by those addicted to alcohol or anything else.

They can't be helped because they don't recognize that they have a problem with addiction. And needless to say, people like that will never achieve anything in their lives. Unless they break free, they will be in drug prison.

Now you may be asking yourself, what do all these have to do with a TV? Well, TV is very similar to drugs. It provokes something very similar to addictive substances because when people watch it, it provokes a pleasant or satisfying sensation, but that pleasant sensation they feel is because of something false. Although there are programs or series that are very healthy, we cannot ignore that most of the content we watch is not real. Whether it's a movie, a soap opera, or some series, it's fake. People have become so addicted to TV that right now, at least in Latin America, even though we have realized that several entertainment programs that boast of being authentic are not, we still watch them. We like to feel those pleasant emotions when we watch the garbage they sell us on TV and that's why we don't care if they are fake situations.

Before you get annoyed with me, let me explain further: Nowadays, we have a youth that is rebellious with their parents, teenagers who think they are adults, who yell at their parents to stay out of their lives, and who have a messy life. Do you know where they saw it and learned about it? Yes, on TV.

LIFE LEAKAGES

Today, in our society, we see twelve and thirteen-year-old boys having sex in such a natural way and pregnant high school girls, most of whom decide to abort their babies. Do you know where they learned it or at least where their sexual appetite was awakened? That's right, by watching television.

Just as drugs destroy a person, television is destroying our homes, our principles, and our values. The bad thing is that television is not just any drug that is sold on the streets, but this drug is in every home and sometimes, in every room. And just to tell you more, do you know where these weird fashions that force children to live like adults come from? Sure, on TV.

And all this happens because, just as drug traffickers do not care how many homes they destroy by selling that crap, so there are unscrupulous people who do not care if they steal the innocence of our children or young people with their television programs.

What they want is to sell and make millions. They do not care about your family, they don't mind putting a sex scene, or that your children also want to experiment with what they see and thus ruin their lives. That is why, dear friend, it is important that you know where all the rebelliousness in adolescents comes from, and if you do not have children you must be well informed so that, when you do have kids, you know that it is not bad that you have a television in your home, what is bad is when you let a seller of inappropriate programs decide what your children will watch. Remember that the leader of your home is you and no one else.

Another negative effect that television has is that it destroys families because it takes away the time that belongs to them. When a person trades the free time that they can spend with the people they love most to be in front of a television, it is very serious because that is how television, like drugs, takes you away from your loved ones. For example, when the family is at home, the children are watching something in one room while the dad is in another, and the family has difficulty getting together to talk because someone is always busy watching their favorite program. Or, on the weekend, the mother often has to go alone to the park with the children because the father has to watch soccer on this device. That is why in this book it is considered as a life leakage.

Another clear resemblance of this object to drugs is violence. For example, in many countries, people complain about violence in the streets and neighborhoods. But if you go to their house, what the entire family, young and old, is watching are those series that are full of violence, drug trafficking, and drugs. This is ironic, isn't it? Complaining because we don't want to see this in our cities and paying to watch it in our living rooms is hypocritical.

But it may be that if we ask one of these families why they watch such violent things if this is precisely what we don't want to see happen, they will use the same excuse that the cocaine addict would use and say something like: "There's nothing wrong with it and I can stop watching it whenever I want to." But we know that's not going to happen.

Now, so as not to come off as being over-the-top or old-fashioned or whatever you are thinking, I encourage you to ensure that in your home there is no such addiction and that no one there is a prisoner of the television. It's very easy to realize, that you can stop

LIFE LEAKAGES

reading this book here and go to your house or your living room or wherever you have a television and tell your family that you have realized that you need to spend more time together and talk more, and that is why you will do the exercise of removing the television for a while, even if it is only for a week. Then you will be able to see who is addicted and you can help them to get out of that addiction.

The advantage of not being tied to television is that you stop living false stories and start forming your own. As I told you with drugs, addicted people don't achieve their dreams because they are dependent on a certain substance.

It is the same with television. As long as we continue to be entertained by watching things that are not real, we will not be able to live our lives that are real. If you or your family manage to get rid of the addiction to television, you will surely have enough time to plan your dreams and goals, you will have time to work on them, and achieve everything you set out to do.

Remember that it's better to be inside the screen. It sure feels better to have someone watching you than for you to be watching someone else. Some TV actors say they hardly watch TV because they don't have time for it. Isn't it ironic that they don't consume their own poison and we're the ones paying money for the garbage they make?

Let me talk a little more about this topic. I have often watched many people gather on the weekend to watch soccer and I have noticed that when someone watches a sport on TV they almost always have the same reactions: they complain and often get angry because the player doesn't throw the ball the way they think they would.

The truth is that it is very different to see the problems and the pressure of the players from outside the screen than from inside.

That's part of life too: Everyone can see your virtues or qualities except yourself, and also, everyone can see the things you are doing wrong except yourself.

You have probably met someone who has bad breath and everyone knows it but him, or you may have heard a mother tell her daughter that she should not marry a man who does not suit her and everyone agreed with the mother except the girl. People who are wasting their time usually don't realize it because of the responsibilities or the pressures of life.

Although television in our times has been a tool that, like cellphones, we could no longer live without, it has become a drug in our homes. Today, we have children addicted to and imprisoned by television, watching someone else's triumphs, and that may be the reason why they will not achieve their goals.

You may think that I am exaggerating or that I am old-fashioned, or maybe you think that what I am saying is not true, that you or your family can stop watching TV any day they want to. Forgive me for making this comparison, but have you ever noticed that when a person has an addiction to wine or some kind of drug, they always say that they can quit whenever they want?

You and I know that this is not so. What happens is that they don't realize they are trapped in a vice that is depleting their lives, they presume and say: "When I want to, I can quit this vice." Well, the same thing may be happening with you or with someone you know.

If this is so, it may be because, without you even realizing it, you have an addiction to being entertained,

LIFE LEAKAGES

an addiction that takes your time and with it, your life. Now, you may be wondering how this could happen. Well, to understand, I will give you an example of when we go to the movies.

Most people love going to the movies when a new movie comes out, so they encourage someone else to go with them to see it. When they get to the theater, they buy popcorn and soft drinks, go to the theater where the screen is, and sure enough, the movie is very good! It has a lot of action scenes; cars colliding, planes crashing, and humans doing incredible maneuvers. Everything is very impressive.

So when the movie is over, those people leave very excited and they get in the car still talking about the experience at the movie theater, about how the cars were crashing, the planes falling; they even talk about the actors and the things they liked about them.

This is because they are very impressed by all that action. If we analyze carefully, we will realize that everything that was watched on that screen is nothing more than the pure imagination of someone who doesn't like to be entertained but likes to entertain others and make millions from it.

All that happened in that movie theater was that people saw the potential of someone who developed their imagination and creativity. If you look at it this way, you will realize that everyone has a hidden potential that, if they develop it, can lead to unimaginable projects, such as a great action movie.

What would happen if you develop that potential? Can you imagine the things you could achieve and what would happen if others saw the greatness, creativity, and power of your imagination?

It can be very addictive to entertain ourselves with the imagination or talent of others and forget about using our own potential or our best talents.

Now let's go back to televisions in homes. Imagine, what would a home be like if instead of being entertained by someone on that small screen, you decided to be the one entertaining others?

If we are not distracted by watching television, we can create great ideas that can later have a positive impact on others, instead of always waiting for someone else to impress us through the screen.

So, I remind you to be careful not to be a victim of the addiction and entertainment of the television media. Remember that you were born to be more than that. By watching a lot of television you are just observing the lives of others, *but you do have your own life*. Watching more news and learning about all the bad things that are happening in the world will not lead you to solve them.

So instead of being impressed with the news you hear, I urge you to get off that couch, get out there and start living your life, and start building your future. Teach those you love that they were born to lead and not to be followers. Be encouraged to create your own life movie and live your own life!

Well, I hope I didn't offend you with this. To finish, I will share with you that one day, when I went to visit my grandfather, I accidentally got a wound on my hand and I asked him to put a bandage on it. But, first, he cleaned the wound with alcohol. That hurt a lot and I told him that I just wanted a bandage and that was it, but he replied that he could not just put the bandage on without cleaning the wound because it would get infected, and then, it would become more serious.

LIFE LEAKAGES

I understood then that sometimes, when we have a problem or are wounded by something in life, we want to be healed without going through the pain, but over time that could hurt us more.

    I mention this because it may hurt or make you uncomfortable, but if we don't entirely heal the things that are draining the life out of you and your family, then, in time, you will regret not having had the opportunity to listen to this advice.

LIFE LEAKAGES

Chapter 5
DISTRACTION

As we mentioned earlier, we know that the biggest problem a person can go through is being imprisoned and not realizing it.

Remember that if you want to become the owner of your own life, first you have to be free. Remember that bondage is everything that prevents you from realizing your dreams or goals.

I once heard that if you don't have plans, dreams, or goals to achieve, you will end up working for those who do.

That is why I encourage you to get out of any prison that holds you back and, in this chapter, I want to talk to you about a very powerful mental barrier that a person can fall into and is almost impossible to get out of. This mental barrier consumes your life and, therefore, also your time. This is also like a drug because most people may even pay a lot of money to get it. It is called *DISTRACTION*.

Distraction is terrible for someone whose desire is to make his dreams come true, and it is even a leak of life because it deprives you of many things. Let me give you an example:

Let's say you got married and you have a nice partner who has given everything for you; however, you may be neglecting her because you are distracted by your friends.

Or suppose you have children. They need you but because you are distracted by friends or co-workers, your children feel neglected.

> I once heard that if you don't have plans, dreams, or goals to achieve, you will end up working for those who do.

To better understand what I am telling you, think back to when you were a child. Perhaps you lived with an absent mom or dad, and you know how terrible this can be; however, your parents were not aware of how distracted they were because, as I mentioned this is an enemy of freedom and even becomes a kind of drug that we spend our money on to get it. In reality, what happens when we become addicted to distraction is that we not only forget about our dreams but also become victims of someone who likes to entertain. When we are captive to distraction, we are no longer happy with the real things. I have known friends who can spend hours, even all weekend, watching movies or reality shows, while their family complains about not having quality time with them.

But as we already said, almost everything we see in movies or TV series is an absolute lie. Nothing we watch or hear is real: Marriages, families, and even action scenes are acted out. That's why I say that we exchange the real for the unreal.

To conclude what I mentioned earlier, people like my friend, who waste their time with the distractions of television, often end up losing their marriage, their children don't feel any benefits of parenthood and they end up doing what their friends teach them: going down the wrong path.

If you realize, it's exactly the same thing that happens to a person who's in prison serving a sentence to the one that's imprisoned in a distraction. This makes their

LIFE LEAKAGES

absence felt at home and sometimes they end up losing their marriage, the respect of their children, and the credibility of their leadership at home.

We need to understand that many areas of our life need to be reviewed to ensure they are not being a leak in our life. It could be that there is something you are doing unconsciously that is taking time out of your life without you realizing it.

For example, almost all of us have the desire to have or achieve something in life. It could be to study for a career and graduate, to buy that luxurious house or that latest model car, or to have a nice family, and we give our complete effort to do our best to achieve this beautiful desire.

Whatever it is you want to achieve or have in life, you are going to have to decide to focus and be careful, very careful of distractions. They can be catastrophic for those who are in the race for success. No matter what you want in life, if you get distracted, you will have a hard time following through. So let me help you understand a little more about this topic.

We live in a world that wherever you go, you will be offered distractions so that, according to what you are told, you won't get bored. And even though there are very nice and very healthy distractions, there are also some that are deadly and will make you dependent on them.

Today, we can see many people entertaining themselves with the lives of some celebrities. They like to watch programs or read magazines that tell them the latest news about their favorite artists, and although, at first glance, it seems that there is nothing wrong with this, it does not take very long to see that they forgot their lives and live off the lives of others.

I have known people who know the names, nicknames, and lives of all the players on their country's soccer team, but they don't even know the name of one of their children's friends.

We can also notice that distraction has invaded us since we were children. Maybe you didn't notice it, but now you can understand it when you see a child wanting to be like a player or wrestler or any famous character. And although this is not bad, it can turn out bad when there is no one to explain to the child that, although it is okay to be a fan of someone, they have to look for their own destiny.

Can you imagine how our lives would have changed if someone had told us that it's okay to admire others, but we don't have to look like anyone else? Because we are unique, we have our own destiny and we should be focused on our purpose. If someone had opened your eyes earlier, don't you think your life would be different?

I assure you that we would have been much more effective, we would have grown up without fear of failure, perhaps focused on our purpose and not distracted or wanting to be something we were not born to be.

Very often I hear parents ask their children why aren't they like their other siblings or their cousins or some other child, and it causes a distraction to this little one, who has to observe how the other is to imitate them and not be themselves. This, dear friend, is to stop living your life to try to live the life of another.

Or sometimes, when I go to lunch with my children at their school, I often hear moms scolding their children. According to them, they are not good because they have very low grades. Today, society has taught us that if a child or teenager has good grades, they are a good

LIFE LEAKAGES

kid but if the grades are low then they are a bad kid.

But we have to realize that grades don't make people, they are just numbers. No one can decide if you are good or bad unless you let them. Some people have told me: "Miguel, I have been very bad since I was a child. I always got bad grades, the teacher told me I was a fool and when I got home, my mother confirmed it by saying: 'Why aren't you as smart as your brother? What do you think about this?" And my answer is always to ask: "Why did you let yourself be fooled? Why were you distracted from your purpose?"

Remember that we were not born to fulfill anyone's expectations, but to live and become warriors to achieve and fight for our goals and dreams. Don't be afraid because we are strong and we were born to win. Don't get distracted by wanting to be someone else, you have your own life and your own destiny. Focus on what you have been given, and let the world run at its own pace.

After all, there are things you can never prevent. You cannot prevent catastrophes from happening in the world, such as if a third world war starts, if there is another earthquake in a certain place, or if there is a rumored world economic crisis, and so on.

> *Don't get distracted by wanting to be someone else, you have your own life and your own destiny. Focus on what you have been given, and let the world run at its own pace.*

There will be things that are going to happen and there is nothing you can do about it. So focus on your purpose. Keep running the race of your life until you win, let nothing distract you, stay focused, and help your loved ones to focus as well. You will always find thousands of reasons to become unfocused and thousands of reasons to get discouraged but remember that you have little time and you cannot be distracted or discouraged. Good things are on the other side of effort; happiness, on the other side of sadness; and joy on the other side of pain. So if you have to suffer and cry, do it. But then get up and do your best because what you want and need is on the other side.

• •
If you have to suffer and cry, do it. But then get up and do your best because what you want and need is on the other side.
• •

We also have to be aware that many of the problems in homes are caused precisely by distractions. Today, we can see parents correcting their children because they are distracted by bad friendships, causing problems, and destroying their lives without realizing it. It is very easy for us as adults to see that teenagers live in such a distracted way. Even if you warn them of the danger, they will think you are crazy because for them, those who are distracted, it's invisible.

But it doesn't only happen in adolescents, it also happens in marriage. Many people today divorce because of infidelity or lack of attention. Although you may have a very good marital relationship and your spouse may be the best and very attentive to you, there will always be distractions, and if you do not learn to focus on the beautiful things that life has given you, you will fall victim to these distractions and they will destroy everything that you have been building for years.

LIFE LEAKAGES

That's why it's important to focus on the people you love and be careful. Remember, you are a winner and cannot be defeated by anyone or anything. The more orderly your home environment and your life is, the more time you will have to live without having a distraction that becomes a life leak.

LIFE LEAKAGES

Chapter 6
YOU HAVE THE CAPACITY TO ACHIEVE ANYTHING

Remember that you were created with all the capabilities to create a very healthy and intelligent environment for you and your loved ones. Each person was given a very great ability called imagination.

Imagination is so powerful that it has no limits and if you use it for good things, it will benefit you in an incredible way.

I heard one day that the moon revolves around the earth, but it is the earth that holds it back and doesn't let it go. I think that, in the same way, in our minds, there are very negative thoughts that go around every day and tell us that we cannot change our current situation, but I am sure that someone put those thoughts there for you.

Today I am here to tell you to let them go and not hold them back. Fill yourself with positive thoughts, use your imagination to create the thoughts you need to achieve what you would like to achieve, and then work hard for it.

Think that every effort is small when it comes to your happiness and the people you love because just as Adam was the first man and was created to take care of the garden of Eden, so you were also commissioned to take care of the home where you live. There you have everything you need to accomplish your purpose.

Create a team with your family, tell them your plans and if you don't have a plan, make one with them. You will see that as a team you will achieve much more and reach your goal sooner. You will see that one person focused on their purpose is more powerful than a thousand distracted ones. You will be effective, successful, and you will be plugging all your life leakages.

6.1 You have what you need

> *One person focused on their purpose is more powerful than a thousand distracted.*

Very often during our lives, we think that we lack many things to be happy or feel fulfilled, or achieve our goals. One of the things that torments a person the most is to feel that something is missing in their life. I have known many who suffer because they feel they do not have the things they need to live a free and happy life.

I am sure that you also know or have known someone who is not happy because they think that something is missing, and although you have tried to encourage them by showing them that they have thousands of reasons to be happy, they can only see what they think is missing.

Let me touch on this subject more deeply:

As I told you before, you were perfectly created without lacking anything. You were given exactly everything you needed, but even so, it always seemed that something was missing and this is so because this world is very selfish and everyone looks for their own interests to benefit them.

LIFE LEAKAGES

For example, in marketing, there are always ads on TV or radio that will try to convince you that you need their products and that if you don't buy from them, you are not fashionable and they may make you feel that you are missing out on something. It is here, dear friend, where many fall into this trap of deception and try to get what they need, according to them, they go into debt to get it and feel whole, but we already know that this is not so.

> *People just do not realize what they have until they lose it.*

We have to believe in ourselves. We may not have everything we want, but we do have everything we need. I know people who are missing some parts of their body like a hand or a foot or both, but they are still very successful because they have understood what I am telling you right now: that you have everything you need.

Speaking of successful people, let's talk a little bit about their success: Today, thanks to the internet, we can watch how they start from scratch and climb to achieve their dreams while others only watch them on TV saying: "How lucky!" But I want to tell you, that good things never come by luck but only as a consequence of the actions of our life.

Because if we take a closer look at things, we can see that both a successful and an unsuccessful person have been given exactly the same thing.

> *Good things never come by luck, everything comes as a result and consequence of the actions of our life.*

If you take a look around your neighborhood right now, you will notice that some live better than others, and maybe you have thought: "I feel sorry for those who have not done as well as these others." But let's analyze why they have not done well. If you notice, they are not at a disadvantage. They live in the same city, they have the same government, they walk the same streets, they breathe the same air, and they have the same twenty-four hours a day. In other words, they have everything they need to live as well as everyone else. But then, why do they live in misery? The answer would be that it is because they believe that they lack something and that is why they cannot get ahead. They believe that they are victims of a society that should help them because they are disadvantaged.

Do you see? That's why, whomever you are and wherever you are, no matter what your situation is right now, I encourage you to believe that you have what it takes to succeed, achieve your dreams and reach your goals.

Don't wait for the solution, act instead.

Dare to believe that you don't need anything else at the moment to start pursuing your dreams, let go of the excuse that you don't have what you need to achieve what you've always dreamed of.

You may be thinking that you lack money or a good job and that if only you had this or that, then you could be the person you would like to be, but that is a delusion.

Today we can look at thousands of cases where millionaires have taken their lives because it is not money that is needed to live a happy and fulfilled life, it is believing that you do not need anything. After all, remember that the rich are not the one who has a lot, but the one who requires the least. It is very easy to get out of poverty, we just have to believe that we do not lack anything and then we can begin to live differently.

LIFE LEAKAGES

A few years ago I met a friend at a job. We talked more and more and got to know each other better and better. One day, I shared my dreams with him and he shared his. We both wanted freedom and not to be tied to a job or a boss. We wanted to have more free time for our families and ourselves. But we didn't know how to do it.

One day we realized that the reason we were living tied to a job was that we needed money and that if we stopped having that need, we would be free. We

Remember that the rich is not he who has much, but he who needs the least.

made a plan, talked to our wives, and told them we wanted to do something crazy. The crazy thing was to save six months of salary and then continue working, but no longer for money; that is, we would tell the boss that he didn't have to pay us, and if he paid us anyway, we would save the money and look for a different way of living. See how crazy it was? And so it came to pass. At first, it was terrible, but then it became so easy to go to work knowing that we weren't doing it for money. The first thing we experienced was that we didn't care if we got fired because we didn't make a living from it anyway. I realized that it was that decision that set us free from work. Then we started saving our salaries because we didn't need them. To buy the basics, we did it differently; for example, we would have a food sale and with the proceeds, we would buy more food.

Suddenly I realized that my savings began to rise incredibly. At work, I felt free and began to demand my rights as a worker because I was no longer afraid of being fired. My co-workers, seeing this, began to see me as a leader and supporter. The company, in turn, promoted me and raised my salary. By this time, my life was only a shadow of what it had been before.

Now, I had a position in the company, a very good salary, and big savings, but the best thing was that I still felt free because I did not depend on the salary, no matter how good it was, I lived in a small apartment, but I felt good, I felt that I had everything I needed, and that gave me a lot of tranquility.

One day, miraculously, I was presented with the opportunity to buy a house. Having my own house, I no longer had to pay rent, now I had fewer worries. Then I started doing what I love the most, which is helping people with addiction or family problems. As a minister, I help them to know their Creator and to be free; I am very passionate about this. So now I can do what I love and what I am most passionate about.

This all started with a small decision and a small effort, but now I wonder what would have happened if I was still thinking that I needed my salary to live. Where would I be right now if I hadn't decided to believe that I am complete and that I don't need anything? I would probably be so busy working that I wouldn't have written this book, and you wouldn't be reading this. So, can you see what one small decision can do?

That's why I encourage you to believe that you are complete, that you lack nothing. If you think this way, you will no longer go into debt to buy unnecessary things. Because you won't need anything, you already have everything you need.

• •

You may not have everything you want,
but you do have everything you need.

• •

LIFE LEAKAGES

Chapter 7
APPEARANCE

Now let's talk about our appearance. Very often I hear people saying: "I don't like my name," "I don't like my nose," "I would have liked to be taller" or "I'm too fat."

These types of thoughts torment people who are trapped in society's system. It's not that they don't like the way they look, but that they can't meet other people's expectations.

For example, a woman may feel ugly, not because she really is, but because her husband tells her so in every argument. Then this woman begins to see flaws in her appearance and torments herself by saying: "If only I were blonder or if only I were thinner or if only I had a different face, I would be prettier." But in reality, she has everything she needs and everything she has is perfect. What happens is that her husband also has these acceptance issues with himself and he reflects that with these kinds of comments to his spouse.

This happens because society sets a standard for how we have to be or how we behave. When we watch a TV soap opera or reality show, we see that everyone is tall, thin, rich, blonde, and elegant. Those who don't have these qualities are labeled as thieves, gang members, bad guys, poor, etc.

But we have to understand once and for all that, almost everything we see on television *is not real*, even the news channels often tell the news in a very exaggerated way, and people eventually believe it and put themselves in a position of misery that they should not be in.

Friend, if this is happening to you, then I want you to know that nothing happens by chance and that, if you are reading this book, it is because your Creator wants you to realize that you already have what you need, that you do not need another color of skin or hair or eyes, that you are already special just as you are and that what defines you is not the commentary of a scoundrel or what the television says. What defines you is what is written in Heaven about you.

I am sure that you were created to be free and happy and you have everything you need to be able to do it. Make up your mind to believe that you can and that it doesn't matter what level of self-esteem you have or what your current situation is to start changing. If you start right now, in a couple of months, you will be a very different person and you will feel happy for having decided to change and not wait to get what you thought you were missing.

Remember that a tree can be very big and provide a lot of shade, but it was not always like that. First, it had to be a seed, then it had to be planted and die as a seed so that a couple of small leaves could come out of its interior that later would become a big tree.

Just like that seed, if you want to grow, you will have to die so that all the greatness that is already in you can come out. This means that you will have to stop doing what has not given you results so far and dare to make the process of change.

Let me explain it better: When the seed is sown, it depends entirely on the natural work of the earth. The earth covers it and the seed dies, but when it becomes a

LIFE LEAKAGES

big tree, many little birds come to it to make their nests, and even people seek the shelter of its shade.

In the same way, you will have to trust the process as if it was the earth and dare to make good habits, even if they do not make sense at first, but the process will do its natural work and little by little, it will bring out the best in you and incredible greatness will come out that will make many seek your shelter and your shadow. This means that many will find in you the shade they need to rest.

7.1 Change is often painful, but worth it

It is worth saying that if you read this and decide to make important decisions in your life that will inevitably bring about change, it is likely that thoughts of fear and doubt will come to your mind, or thoughts that will tell you that all this is not for you because you were born into a broken family or because, perhaps, you grew up without a father or maybe your mother abandoned you.

Anyway, many things may come to your mind, even some that will cause you pain because of the wounds provoked from the past. But it is precisely here where you have to remember that it is through pain that people come into the world.

Let's take a look at two examples of this:

    1. First, in childbirth, we see a mother suffering a lot from the physical pain of giving birth to something she will love for the rest of her life. This means that sometimes, if you want to get something you love, you will have to suffer and cry because, at that moment, that is the only way we can get something we love.

2. The child being born is putting all its strength into making its way to life. Although childbirth is risky and mother and child can die, at this moment the two are fighting with all their strength and forming a bond of love that they will enjoy together forever.

This is how you come to life amidst the screams and pain of a mother giving birth, but then this same mother is filled with happiness as she looks at her baby and forgets the pain. In the same way, it is making a change for you. It may hurt to give up bad habits and start doing things you're not used to; you may have to get away from friends or family members who always make you feel like garbage. All of that hurts, but just like a mother giving birth, you too will receive the result of your pain and you can happily say that it was worth the effort.

Now, perhaps a thought may come to you saying that you cannot begin to value yourself because you are not capable or you lack something, but I encourage you not to continue believing that lie. Remember that you were created by divine will, that you are made perfect by a perfect being, and that you have everything you need. If you lack something, then the Creator will give it to you.

•••••••••••••••••••••••••••••••
The book of Romans 8:32 says that God, "having given us his Son, he would not give us everything else too?"
•••••••••••••••••••••••••••••••

So, we can be sure that if we don't have what we want now, it's because we don't need it, but if you start walking towards your purpose, the things you need will appear.

LIFE LEAKAGES

When the great leader, Moses delivered the nation of Israel from the slavery of Egypt, he did so by divine command, but he was never told that the sea would open, that a cloud would cover them from the heat in the desert, that light would warm them by night, or that manna would fall from heaven.

All that came in due time. The sea did not open until they came to the sea. The cloud and the light were not in the wilderness, they did not appear until they got there. The manna did not appear until they ran out of food.

Now, all these miracles would not have happened if they had not decided to leave the slavery of Egypt. If they had waited until they had the necessary things to make the decision, none of this would have happened. If they had thought that it was crazy, that the dessert was too hot, too cold, or that they would not find food, or how they would cross the sea, they would never have obtained their freedom.

If you start walking towards your purpose, then the things you need will appear.

And that's life: sometimes you have to make decisions, even though you don't know where you are going. This is like when you are driving your car on the highway and you can't see the end of the road, but only the distance your eyes can reach, and as you go along you can visualize the part of the road you couldn't see before. In the same way, the doors of opportunity will open as soon as you are in front of them.

No longer live a stagnant life but dare to walk towards a new life full of changes and miracles, without fears or limitations, where you can be fulfilling your purpose on this earth and taking advantage of every minute and every moment of your valuable and beautiful life.

7.2 A few recommendations

Regarding the earlier things, in conclusion, it is necessary to make the most of the free and conscious time that we have.

> *The Bible says in Ephesians 5:16 to make the best of time because the days are evil*

This means that every day you will be presented with thousands of reasons to waste your time, but you must be wise to make the years you will spend on this pilgrimage of your life in this world pay off. Knowing that we spend many years sleeping, strive not to do more than we need to. Normally, people sometimes sleep long hours in the morning because sleeping is also a pleasure that causes a lot of satisfaction, but if you are aware that while you are sleeping longer than you need, you are losing time of your life, I am sure that you will rest only as much as your body needs and not as much as your flesh wants.

Also, it is important to note that no successful person who has ever existed has ever recommended sleeping too much. This is the reason why some can do more than others: Although we all have twenty-four hours a day, only a few think about how to take advantage of them and make the most of them, while others think that the more free time they have, the more they will take advantage of it to take a nap or rest a little.

LIFE LEAKAGES

In most companies, there are two types of workers. First, there are the most common ones, those who spend their time watching the clock, anxiously waiting for the time to go home to rest, watch TV, or sleep.

But then there are the others who know how to make the most of their time. Time does not torment them, they are the kind of people who enjoy their work. They don't look at the clock all day, you always see them full of energy, and when it's time to leave they are the last to go. But when they leave, they don't go to watch TV or sleep or waste their time, just the opposite. They are still working, but now on their own goals or maybe on a business, they are doing or an invention. If they had nothing to do, you would probably see them reading a book because these people like to learn. After all, they know and believe a truth that has already been forgotten: *the day you stop learning, you stop living.*

That is why it's important for you to learn that if you make good use of your time, you will also be able to do more things, have more opportunities to achieve your goals and dreams, and live your life more efficiently.

The day you stop learning is the day you stop living.

For example, if you make an effort and get up an hour earlier in the morning, just one hour a day in a year, that would be three hundred and sixty-five extra hours.

This is approximately fifteen days, which means that you will have fifteen extra days per year. This will give you an advantage and put you in front of many just by taking advantage of an extra hour a day to exercise, read, cook breakfast, or do whatever you want to invest in. It will make you a better person and will greatly benefit you, so much so that in a couple of years of doing this routine, you will be amazed at what a small decision and a small change can achieve in a person's life.

7.3 About the job

There is much to say about a job, but nothing new that you don't already know. Remember that when you work for someone else you are selling your life. That is why you must not fall into the deception of riches. One day, I learned that no one in history has ever become rich or a millionaire by working; that is, there's not a job that will give you financial freedom. What can free you from the schedule of a job is what you already have inside you. When you start working on your ideas and developing your potential, you will earn money in a way where you no longer have to trade your time for money.

You have to believe that things are made for you and not you for things. Remember that you are a person, you are not a work machine. I understand very well that sometimes we have no choice and we have to work overtime; this is not the problem, the problem begins when we leave the things we love because we have to work.

I have known of many occasions where, one morning, a man gets up to go to work and while he is getting ready to leave, his wife with a very anguished voice tells him not to go to work because our child was sick during the night and is very ill. But the husband almost always says: "You take care of it, woman, I have to go to work." Do you see? The problem begins when we leave what we love the most to be distracted by a job that chains us and makes us lose sight of what is most important.

LIFE LEAKAGES

I'm not saying that it's bad to work. What I'm trying to say is that you can do better than that. You have to understand that you can't trade the best you have for a job; the job can end at any time, but you will always want your family by your side. That's why I encourage you to look inside yourself. I am sure that somewhere in your heart or some corner of your mind you must have a creative idea that you need to develop.

This idea can be like a seed. Because it looks so small, you think it is not worth saving and investing time in cultivating it, but if you dare to do it, soon this idea will become strong and will become your livelihood. It doesn't matter the size of your dream or your idea, what truly matters is the effort or time you dedicate to making it grow. You have to believe in yourself and believe in your potential, don't wait for others to do it. You are responsible for your life, fight against circumstances, against those things that make you think that it is not worth trying, and make your dream come true. Dare yourself!

LIFE LEAKAGES

Chapter 8
TIME-WASTING ACTIVITIES

On your life's journey, you will always find hundreds of reasons to keep busy. You can be entertained on your cell phone just wasting time, on TV, at parties, or with illicit pleasures.

But, my friend, you have to think that you are not going to get anything done if you just keep busy. In fact, everybody is busy with different things, and we can always hear somebody say: "I am busy," and we think that person is succeeding, but they are not because, as I told you, everybody is busy with something, and it may be in vain thinks like the ones I already mentioned.

But you don't need to be busy, you need to be *productive*. Do you know what I mean? For example, you can be busy watching your cell phone, but you can change that and instead of wasting your time on this device, you can be productive watching your cell phone. You will be doing the same thing, but with a different purpose. Nowadays, there is so much business being done on the internet that a cellphone has become the most useful tool to do it, and if you are not making money during the time you are on your cell phone, then you don't need it because if you are not profiting from it, someone else is profiting from you through your cell phone.

When you are only using your cellphone to be on social networks or to play games, the creators of those applications are making money from you. If you think about it, in your hands you have a gold mine that can produce money, either for you, if you know how to use it, or for someone else who, even if you don't know him, every time you go to pay your mobile service bill, a part of it goes to him. Now you see that being busy doesn't allow you to earn? What you really need is to be productive by doing something worthwhile.

You can also be very entertaining and waste time with certain friends, party friends who, although you have a good time with them and have a great appreciation for them, are people without dreams and goals. They do not even have an idea of what they are alive for and, as my grandmother used to tell me when she wanted to advise me, "Miguel, hang out with wolves and they will teach you how to howl." The bad thing about spending too much time with friends at parties and other things is that we become precisely more and more like them. So you have to be smart, take some time, and look at the lifestyle of your friends because that is exactly the lifestyle that you will also have in the future.

I know it feels good to have many friends, but life is not a game. We have limited time, so it is very much recommended that you surround yourself with people who are better than you, but most of all who are in the position you want to be in because they already know the way to get there. But you have to know that these people only hang out with quality people. You don't need to be in the same position as them to be their friend because wealth is not measured by what you have but by who you are, and if you are not whom you want to be, then start seeing yourself not as you are, but as the person, you can become.

The wise Solomon once said: "Better is the end of a thing than the beginning."

LIFE LEAKAGES

So prepare yourself, read books, learn as much as you can so you can have the mindset of a successful person and, even if you have not achieved your goals yet, you will be able to live as if you have already achieved them.

One day, a friend told me that when a group of people goes exploring, the first difficulty they encounter is finding water they can drink. To do this, they do something very simple but at the same time incredible because of how effective it is. They look for an area where there are monkeys or chimpanzees and pretend to drop a small bucket of salt. Since monkeys are very curious, they immediately ran over to pick it up and eat it. Once they do, they feel thirsty from the effects of the salt and the first thing they do is go to where the water is. All the people have to do is follow the monkeys and they will get to safe drinking water. So it is with the people who have already found success; they are the support that will guide you on the right path. Don't be envious or angry with them, but rather listen to them and watch what they do because, after all, they know the way to what you need.

> • • • • • • • • • • • •
> *Wealth is not measured by what you have but by who you are. If you are not whom you want, then start seeing yourself not as you are but as the person, you can become.*
> • • • • • • • • • • • •

8.1. Enemies that damage your destiny

Now I will show you some enemies that are like parasites that cling to a person's life and can be hard to get rid of.

I was born in a very small town in central Mexico. I grew up learning to till the land and feed animals because that is what my parents and grandparents did. Of the animals we raised, there was one thing that always attracted my attention: When a steer in the herd began to lose weight and stopped growing, my grandfather said it was because it had parasites. It could be worms, lice, or some other kind of pest, but the truth is that you couldn't see any of them, you could only tell because the animal stopped growing and putting on weight. For a farmer this is terrible, but my grandfather immediately went to the veterinarian and bought medicine that killed the parasites no matter what they were. He put this medicine in the animal's food and a miracle happened. In a matter of days, the steer was stronger and fatter, and it kept growing.

But what attracted my attention was how a parasite as small as lice or worms could impede the growth of such a strong bull, which in size is not even comparable because, next to it, the parasite is like nothing.

One day I asked my grandfather how this happened. He explained that the parasites eat the nutrients that make the animal grow and that, if they are not killed, the animal, no matter how strong it looks, will end up dying from malnutrition.

Not that I want to compare you to an animal, but just like these bulls, humans are also affected by certain types of parasites that drain their energy and begin to rob them of the nutrients they need to live. These parasites are very dangerous enemies that if not detected in time can be killing you little by little without you realizing it.

So here I will introduce you to some of the most common ones. So, if you think that some of the ones I mention below are attacking you, then may this book come to be like that medicine, and may it enter your mind so that you can kill every enemy parasite that can drain your life.

LIFE LEAKAGES

8.2 Fear

A very common enemy is fear. In fact, because of how dangerous it is, it has been talked about a lot to prevent people, but here we will learn its attack strategies so that, if you think it is attacking you, you can detect it and put an end to it.

The first thing we must understand is that today there are many types of fear but here we will only talk about two.

The fear that is not a parasite and that we all have by nature: is that fear that a horror movie causes, for putting an example, or when you are afraid of falling somewhere or when someone hides and scares you. That is part of us and we feel it by nature, like the fear of snakes or spiders.

This fear is like pain, they are reactions of our body that ensure our survival, as basic instincts with which we come into the world to survive. If, for example, a deer were not afraid of the lion, it would be eaten by it. Or if we couldn't feel pain when we were burned by fire, we would stay there until we burned to death. In modern psychology, this is called a phobia, but it is natural and we cannot change it. That is why feeling fear or pain is not bad. The problem is when it becomes another kind of harmful fear. Let's talk about the fear that is not part of us, the one that is like a parasite, and when it sticks to us it is very difficult to get it out of our lives.

This enemy is very cunning, it disguises itself in many ways so that you do not recognize it, but here are some of its effects so that, if you feel any of them, you will know that this parasite is in you: One of the disguises that this enemy uses is called PRUDENCE.

Yes, I know it sounds crazy because it is wise to use prudence. But many times, people do not do something in their lives thinking that it is because they want to act prudently, but in reality, what is holding them back is the fear that things will not go well.

For example, let us say that Camilo has been working for ten years for a company where he earns one hundred dollars a day, and suddenly another company hears about him and knows that he is an excellent worker, so they call him and offer him one hundred and fifty dollars a day. If Camilo has been conquered by this enemy, he will not accept the offer and will say that it is too risky, that it would be imprudent to risk leaving a known place to go to another place he doesn't even know. I am sure you know someone like this, but in reality, what happens to Camilo is that he is afraid of change and the unknown.

Fear keeps us in one place, prevents us from taking risks in life, and makes us think that something can be too good to be true. The worst thing is that it makes us conformist and mediocre.

Let me tell you, my friend, that there is nothing worse than being in mediocrity. That is, we dare not start anything new for fear of losing (even if we have nothing to lose).

We also don't want to end up with anything because we are terrified of being at zero and starting all over again. But we have to understand that if we don't start with new projects, new things won't come into our lives either and that it is worth getting rid of fear and daring to make decisions that move us from where we are, whether it works or not, we will never lose because if you dare to take a step forward, if you manage to step in a safe place, you will realize that you have already moved further! And if you fall, then you will learn that this is not the way. You will have learned a new experience and it will truly help you even more because it is in the difficult moments that you learn.

During my life, I've had very good moments. I really like being in those moments, but I have to recognize that what I've learned during my life has not been during the good moments but during the bad ones. It has been during the moments that I have stumbled in life, where I have felt the rejection of many and the abandonment of all, where I have learned to trust in God and to get up without the help of anyone because that is how we humans learn to walk: falling down and getting up. It doesn't matter how many times we fall, but how many times we get up. Today, we walk without any fear because when we learned to walk we did not care about the pain of falling. The desire to walk was stronger than the pain and fear of falling. That is why we got up again and again, as many times as necessary until we stood upright.

We have to believe that fear will not be able to control us and although understandably, we are afraid of making mistakes, we have to think that after all we are human and humans make mistakes, but we keep trying, again and again, until we get it right.

I remember there was a time when my wife Jazmín and I were very worried about my son Michael. We wanted him to be well and hoped that nothing would happen to him. When he got sick with the flu or a fever, we were alarmed and desperately rushed to the hospital. But one day, while my wife and I were having dinner at a restaurant with my brother and his wife, I received a call that my son had been hit by a car and was unconscious in a helicopter on his way to the hospital.

When I ended the call my skin color changed, and everyone noticed. My wife, worried, asked me what was wrong, and I didn't hold back any longer and told them the news. After urgently paying the bill, we set off like mad for the hospital. We were going so fast that we arrived before the helicopter. When it finally arrived, they took my son to the hospital. The doctor said that Michael was unresponsive and had been unconscious for a long time. After X-rays, we were told that Michael had one lung completely gone and the other was full of blood, several veins in his brain had burst, there was bleeding inside his head and he had many broken bones.

I don't have to explain to you how we felt. I imagine you know what a moment like that is like. The next day many people from the church went to pray for him, some called each other and made a prayer chain, and that is when the miracle happened that the doctors could not understand.

Now Michael is healthy and strong, but Jazmín and I are no longer the same. We are stronger now and we don't worry like we used to. If we looked at the flu as a threat, after what we went through and suffered, now we see it as a joke.

I am telling you this to tell you that bad times always make you stronger. I don't know what you are afraid of or what opportunity you are letting go for fear that something will not go well, but I encourage you to get rid of that parasite of fear. Take courage, take a chance, walk forward, and think that it is better for you to stumble and get up like a brave man than to stand and do nothing like a coward.

> *It is better for you to stumble and get up like a brave man than to stand and do nothing like a coward.*

LIFE LEAKAGES

Chapter 9
SECURITY DOES NOT EXIST

Let us begin by recognizing that, most of the time, millions of people are stuck in fear, hoping that times will change in their favor, so they will be encouraged to live their lives as they would like to. This happens because we like to feel secure and are, therefore, terrified of insecurity. But by now, we should have realized that security does not exist.

Sometimes fear makes us think that a little is better as well as safe and that it is better to be secure in what we have. But that is a lie because as long as we live on this earth, we have to realize that security does not exist. Think about it for a few minutes. We are very dependent on a system that the government runs; if something goes wrong, the economy will collapse and we will all pay for it. When you drive on the road you are exposed to a drunk driver and have a terrible accident. If you talk or get close to someone, they can give you one of the thousands of diseases that exist. A thief can break into your house when you are not there, and we could go on and on. Do you realize that safety is just a nice wish?

As we already said, there is no such thing as security, so if you are alive, you run many risks. So, I invite you to experiment with new things, to set up the business you have always wanted to have, to give yourself an opportunity, and start a new way of working. Because if you keep doing what your ancestors did, you will have the same results, or if you keep working the same way others do when they don't have results, what makes you think that you will? So dare to get rid of your fear of risks, remember that prudence and fear are two very different things.

> As the famous quote says: "Insanity is doing the same thing over and over again, expecting different results."

I have known people who have spent their lives regretting because they did not dare to take certain risks. I recently talked with someone who had a lot of marital problems. After a while, he declared himself guilty of all the hell he was going through. He told me that he married without loving his wife. He was in love with a girl, but he never confessed it to her for fear of her rejection. So when a brave man came along who did take the risk, he got the girl and married her. The other boy later married, but he never stopped loving the one who was his first love. And I ask myself: How many people like him are there in the world suffering for not taking the risk? Or how many people live suffering for love, for not wanting to take the risk of forgiving and giving another chance?

That's why it's important that whatever the situation, you take the risk. After all, you already have the "no." What would happen if you took the risk and got a "yes"? Your life would change, wouldn't it?

Today we can see men and women suffering for love because things didn't go well in their marriage. Maybe one of the two was unfaithful or one simply lied about something, and the other is offended and cannot forgive because they don't want to take the risk of being let down again. There are also many unhappy marriages

LIFE LEAKAGES

because one has had a hard time letting go of one's parents and always tries to please them more than their partner because they don't want to take the risk of their family saying that they were abandoned.

Going a little deeper, today couples don't get married and only live in a common-law marriage for fear that things won't work out and they will have to divorce later. Because of this fear, a pretty girl gives up her dream of walking down the aisle in white, being given away by her father, and experiencing that rich feeling of a real wedding. Sure, I know you may say I'm talking old fashioned, but whether we want to realize it or not, until now walking down the aisle in white is still every woman's dream, but out of fear these things have stopped happening. Friend, whether you are married and you are the offended party, the one who doesn't want to get away from the parents, or you are about to live in a common-law marriage to avoid a wedding for fear that in the future things won't work out, I encourage you not to be afraid to forgive and try again. After all, if they fail you again, the good thing will be that it wasn't you who failed and that you are a brave person who takes chances.

What would happen if you took the risk and got a "yes"? Your life would change, wouldn't it?

When someone gets married, the first person in your life is your spouse, no longer your mom or dad. Have the courage to be independent, and cut the umbilical cord that keeps you attached to your parents because now you have to follow your destiny. Don't be afraid to fail because even if that happens, you will enjoy it, having been encouraged to step out of the boat of security and walk courageously.

You've probably heard the hackneyed phrase "fight for your dreams." But success is achieving the things you would like to do, and I know very well that you want to do things right. So, dare to fulfill your dream of walking down the aisle with the love of your life. Don't be afraid, take the risk, and then fight to carry on the beautiful institution of marriage.

9.1 What people will say

Another disguise that the fear parasite often uses and that is worse than the one I mentioned before is what people will say.

This simple and short phrase is the cause of people dying as if they had never lived. Fear uses this disguise so that people do not feel cowardly, but cautious, hiding behind what people will say. For example, if you are a person who plans to do great things in this life's wanderings, and you have great ideas in your head that you could put into practice to achieve your goals soon, but you find yourself stuck even after all that, you are probably being held back by this terrible enemy known as "what will they say?" Maybe you think you will be laughed at or that no one will believe in your ideas or your plans, or maybe you think it is not worth the risk because if you fail, what will others say about you?

For a while, this enemy kept me, prisoner, too. I remember that I drove a very old car. It was a little unpainted, the engine often spilled water and oil, and sometimes it took a long time to start. For that reason, when I arrived at a meeting or work, I always looked for the farthest parking place, where no one could see the car I was driving, to avoid what people would say.

LIFE LEAKAGES

I preferred to be seen walking and when I left, I would wait for everyone to leave so I could be the last one to get into my old car.

As I was driving, I thought that I could buy a new car and I would no longer have this kind of worries so, not many days later, I had the opportunity to purchase a very good car with zero miles and at a very good price. I felt happy, I drove just for the sake of driving on different streets of the city, and I was delighted to hear the sound of the powerful engine. I thought: "At last, my shame is over, now I will never again have to be ashamed of the car I drive." Or so I thought. When I arrived at the next scheduled meeting, I was embarrassed to be seen arriving in a new and expensive car. I wondered what they would say. They would say that I was smug, that I just wanted to humiliate others, among many other things. I decided to go to the same distant parking lot where no one would look at the car I was arriving in, and I did so for a long time.

Now, do you understand? It wasn't the old car or parking far away that had me tied up in shame, it was actually the fear of what people would say, and I had to realize that it doesn't matter what car we drive, what clothes we wear, or what brand of shoes we have on. This enemy doesn't care about any of that. As long as you don't get rid of it, it will deprive you of being yourself.

I once heard it said that in war, the people in charge of training soldiers repeat to them a very old and very well-known phrase: "kill or be killed." Sure, I know it's a phrase that sounds very violent and very ugly, but when it comes to our enemies, it is nothing less than reality. Likewise, if you don't end your fear of what people will say, it will finish you.

This is what I had to do when I decided that I would no longer care what others might think of me arriving with a new car to my meetings because I can be responsible for what I do and what I say, but not for what other people perceive or imagine about me. When I decided to put an end to this enemy, I was able to enjoy more of what I had achieved by buying my new car.

Once I shed this enemy, I realized that not only had I grown as a person, but this change meant that I was also able to inspire others to achieve some long-desired goals.

> ....
> *I can be responsible for what I do and what I say but not for what other people perceive or imagine about me.*
> ....

So we can say that another advantage we have in getting rid of this enemy is that we can encourage others to do the same.

Although material things do not make you a better person, it is important not to be afraid to strive for them.

Remember that a blind man cannot lead a blind man, nor can a hungry man feed a hungry man. You have to break from conformity to show what you can achieve and that it is possible to have a comfortable and dignified life as a result of your honest effort, without having to do illicit work.

9.2 In personal areas

What people will say is like a deadly weapon of fear. I have known married men where their life is hell because they have a wife who does not respect them and sometimes has even been unfaithful, but they live tied to her for fear of what people will say. They believe that if they separate, society will judge them, society will mock them, and they will live with their pride and dignity trampled on.

LIFE LEAKAGES

That is why these men prefer to pretend that they are strong and that they have everything under control, but they are truly afraid of being mocked and pretend that they have a lifestyle that meets the expectations of the family or society, even if that leads them to suffer by living a lie, just existing, without living a dignified life.

This case also applies to women who prefer to live with their partners even though they know they are unfaithful. Do you know someone like this? Do you realize that no matter who you are, fear of what people will say affects us all?

Not to mention the thousands of women who live enduring domestic violence by a wretch who beats them and humiliates them even in front of their children. These women suffer almost always throughout their lives and do not dare to separate, not out of fear, but because of what people will say. I have been to several funerals where a woman was killed by her husband in a moment of jealousy or drunkenness, and when I ask what her life was like, they always tell me that long before the tragedy there was already a lot of violence, but that she did not want to separate and made the excuse that she put up with it all for her children.

It sounds as if this person is a good mother, but think about it, does a good mother want her children to grow up in an environment full of violence and then begin to hate their father? One of them will hit the father, the father will hit the mother and so it will become a cycle full of hatred, resentment, and misfortune. It is here where we should realize that a mother would never want that for her children and that the reason she avoids a separation is for fear of what people will say, even if it costs her life.

LIFE LEAKAGES

Chapter 10
MURDERED FOR FEAR OF WHAT THEY WILL SAY

You may still think this all sounds far-fetched, but I want to take the liberty to expose this terrible enemy. According to some statistics made by Life-News, in the United States, 3,300 abortions are performed every day and 137 abortions every hour, this has led to say that the leading cause of death is abortion.

Now, I know that we can have thousands of beliefs about this issue, but we can never deny that after a woman has an abortion, no matter what she believes about it, she will feel the aftereffects of murder. In fact, many do not resist it and end up taking their own lives, and some others carry this pain and guilt for the rest of their lives. As I told you, this is a very difficult subject, and if you have had an abortion or were complicit in convincing your girlfriend or wife to do this, you know what I am talking about. But I'm not saying this to make you feel bad, on the contrary, I'm saying it so you can see how powerful the fear of what people will say is.

• •
We cannot deny that a man or woman who decides to end the life of their own child does so out of fear of what people will say.
• •

Do you see it now? Do you realize what fear of what people will say can do?

Now, if the statistics are true and abortion is the main cause of death, and it is practiced out of fear of what people will say, then this parasitic enemy must be banished from our lives forever. It doesn't matter if it is their fault that we have committed atrocities, we still have time to change and not live in fear and to teach the people we love to dare to live free, without fear of what others may think of them.

Dare to believe that you were not born to fulfill anyone's expectations. No one can decide the person you have to be. The next time someone tries to kill your dreams or your goals, remind them that they didn't create you, and therefore don't know what you are capable of.

I encourage you that if you are going to believe anyone about what they say about you, then you better dare to believe your Creator. He knows what you are capable of because he is the one who gave you those capabilities.

One day, someone told me a story. At the time when motor cars were just becoming popular, a man was standing by the side of the road with his car broken down. Although several auto mechanics had tried to fix the fault to start the car, none had succeeded. Just as the owner was about to give up and had decided to throw it away like a tin can, a very new, very elegant car pulled up and a well-dressed man got out and went to him and asked him what had happened. The owner, in desperation, told him that the car had an unknown fault that no one had been able to find. The elegant man asked to allow him to fix it, but the owner only

LIFE LEAKAGES

laughed mockingly and replied: "My friend, professional technicians have already come and have not been able to fix my car and from the way you are dressed it is obvious that you know nothing about this, so go away and leave me alone."

But the elegant man just moved a couple of wires and started it. The owner, very surprised, asked him: "Man, who are you and how did you fix my car?"

The fancy man replied: "My friend, I'm Henry Ford. I designed this engine and I built it. I am its creator and that's why it's not hard for me to know how to fix it."

Just like Henry Ford and the engine, you also have a Creator who knows very well what may be happening to you. The bad thing is that you have turned to inexperienced people who do not even know about their own lives, but I assure you that your Creator knows very well your weaknesses and your capabilities. He is the one who created you and put talent in you. Just as he gave you gifts; he gave you everything you need so that you do not depend on the approval of others.

Therefore, when you are convinced that it was God and not people who created you, then you will say: "I am not afraid of what they may say about me because I am not what someone says I am, nor am I what others think I am; therefore, no one can decide my destiny. My future was already predestined by my Creator. He put all things in my favor and I'm not afraid that someone will think otherwise because I'm not afraid of what people will say."

10.1 Let go of your past

When a person dies, he becomes part of the past, his life becomes just a finished story and he will never again have something new to say.

That also happens when a person gets stuck in a past problem. Today, there are millions of people who were physically or sexually abused as children and still feel guilty or angry about it or are in a relationship with someone unfaithful that ruined the marriage and the offended person was devastated and even after many years cannot get over it.

The truth is that no matter what you have lived through in the past, whether good or bad, you have to let go of it so that you can live your life in the present. No one who intends to win a race can run looking backward. You have an entire race ahead of you, called life and I encourage you to live it but keep in mind that you will need to let go of your past. Even if it was very bad or very good, there is no longer anything there for you. You have to move on with your life and move forward.

As Eleanor Roosevelt once said,
"Yesterday is history, tomorrow is a mystery,
today is a gift, that's why it's called the present."

It's a very accurate phrase and although it was so successful at the time, the truth is that today, we see so many people trapped in their past, thinking about the things that went wrong, the relationship that didn't work out, the money that was lost, or resenting life for a loved one that is gone, that they can't truly enjoy their present.

LIFE LEAKAGES

The past may have been very bad, but you cannot be tied to it. As I told you, the stories of the dead are in the past and you are still alive. So encourage yourself to live in your present and forget everything that happened, all those things that one day hurt you and that somehow marked your life. Do not let enemies such as hatred or resentment keep you tied up and not living, you can leave your past and focus on your present.

I have met many people stuck in their past who tell how well they did, the battles they won, and the good times they had. Listening to them is very exciting because the past was very good, but that good becomes bad when they can't get anything new because they are savoring the things of the past. So I can say that it doesn't matter if the past was good or bad, it is an enemy that can keep you imprisoned so that you don't do anything new.

The truth is that we can say that the past is very tempting and we even like to think about what happened and we even feed the memories that harm us and kill us little by little.

I have seen many people who, after losing a loved one are never the same, and of course, it is well understood that this happens because of the love we have for someone who left, but if they could learn to let go of the past, they could go on with their lives. I have seen very closely people who, after burying a loved one, begin to die also of grief, and only a few months later someone is burying them because that same grief that anchored them in the past made them sick and killed them.

One day I watched a documentary about how anchors are used on ships, and I learned that they are essential, especially on giant ships because they are very heavy and very difficult to break.

I also learned that when a ship is about to begin a voyage it needs to weigh anchor. If it doesn't, two of the most dangerous things can happen. One is that the ship may have trouble moving forward, and the other is that the anchor may capsize or damage the ship. It struck me that, despite the size of these immense and gigantic ships, a small anchor can prevent them from moving forward or can even severely damage them. I thought then that in our lives there can sometimes be anchors that stop us.

God made us strong, filled us with talent, gave us gifts, and put great potential in us. It is said that we are God's masterpiece. However, no matter how strong you are or how much potential there is in you, if you have an anchor in your past, you will not be able to move forward into your future. If an anchor in the past does not allow you to enjoy your present, you will be unable to enjoy or forge your future or your destiny. That is why it is very important that you lift those anchors that are in your past and maybe you haven't noticed them.

LIFE LEAKAGES

Chapter 11
POSITIVE THOUGHTS

Watch your thoughts because a person is defined by what they think. This means that as your thoughts are, so will you be. In other words, you will become what you think.

That is what was said by a man named Solomon who, according to the Bible, was such a wise man that there was none like him before him and it was believed that there would be none after him.

> *He said in the book of Proverbs 23:7,*
> *"For as he thinks within himself, so he is."*

We can assume that our mind is like a battlefield where you fight for the lifestyle you will have; that is, usually the mind always thinks the worst. For example, surely you have experienced that when you go to a job interview, your mind may be telling you: "You're not going to get it," "This is too much for you," "You are not good for this," "The other person who is waiting to be interviewed is better than you," "Go away before you ruin it," etc.

Another clear example of how the mind almost always thinks the worst is when a loved one is late getting home and it's already dark. You can almost always worry that something bad has happened to them.

The mind has two types of thoughts, and they are like two wolves, one positive and one negative. The negative one will always seek to eat the food of the other, getting stronger every time you think something negative, and increasingly weakening the positive one.

But why is it almost always thought that it was something bad and not something good that is causing the delay of this loved one?

I remember that, when I was a kid, I saw my mother cry a lot of times, worried sick because my dad wouldn't arrive home. She always said that surely something bad had happened, but then my father would arrive home as if nothing had happened and even happier than usual because of the effects of a few shots of alcohol. The interest of this story is that it is repeated almost daily; I mean, almost every day my father would arrive late and also almost every day my mother believed that something bad had happened to him.

Why can't we trust in our beloved ones instead of living with fear? Indeed we always must be on the lookout for them, but we cannot let our life go away in worries that don't exist.

That's why it's important to know that, by nature, our mind always will want to conduce us to failure, worries, or anxiety. If you understand that, now you will have to fight against yourself to not be a victim of your own mind, you have to train it to think only the best. Is in this field of battle where you will have to win every day to have only positive thoughts.

Besides, the things that will happen will happen, and the ones that won't, even if you want them to happen, won't happen. So I encourage you to train your mind to think only the best.

LIFE LEAKAGES

The mind creates negative and very bad thoughts to make you think the worst, but remember that your future depends on what your mind thinks.

On the other side, we can say that thought are like seeds and our mind is like a fertile soil that will germinate these seeds not caring if they are good or bad.

That's why your thoughts should always be good and productive. If you are only thinking that you can't, then you won't be able to do it. If you are thinking that you are poor, then you will always live in poverty.

I live in the United States and, in this country, it has been proven that the hardest working people are Latinos. But it is also very clear that Latinos are the poorest in the country (but of course, there are exceptions). If, as Latinos, we work more but we are also the ones who live more in need, we can assume that it is not only about working hard to get ahead, but it also requires changing the way of thinking. If we only work without changing our mentality, we will always want to live like rich people but think like poor people. Dear friend, let me tell you that real change starts from the inside. If we first change our thoughts of poverty and limitations, the rest begins to come true.

I can be almost certain that you have watched the Tarzan movie. In fact, many of us grew up watching his cartoons.

The movie of Tarzan's life was about how he thought he was a gorilla because when he was little, he grew up in the jungle and a gorilla raised him. As he grew up with the rest of the gorillas, he began to walk, eat, think, and consequently, live as gorillas live.

> *The mind creates negative and very bad thoughts to make you think the worst, but remember that your future depends on what your mind thinks*

Now, we have to note that he could walk, eat, and think like a person, but he didn't know it because he had been raised like gorillas.

Like Tarzan, we have to recognize that many people, including ourselves, may have grown up with people that have a mentality and culture that was unavoidable to adopt. Just as Tarzan began to think like a gorilla, we too may think that we were born to be poor all our lives and that we will have to make do with what is necessary. This is because from the time we were very young we listened to mom and dad talk about poverty. In fact, I can respectfully state that many of us grew up in a home where people did not have a complete education; therefore, we grew up just like them and we only cared about survival.

One day, a friend told me a small but very interesting legend. Once upon a time, a sheepherder who was tending his flock near a small but very beautiful river was looking after his sheep to make sure he was not missing any when suddenly he heard some noise, like those of a small lion. Filled with curiosity, he approached the place where the faint roars were coming from and suddenly saw that it was a lion cub that had gotten lost from its mother. The shepherd thought that if he ignored it and left it there, the cub would die, and thought it best to take it with him to save its life. However, deep inside, he worried about what would happen when the lion grew up because he was a sheepherder and lions eat sheep.

But in the end, his good heart was stronger and he did not want to leave the cub to its fate. He took it in his right hand, hugged it, and returned it to the sheep. After a while, the shepherd realized that the little cub was hungry and thought: "How am I going to feed this poor animal? It's too small to eat meat, I have to get milk." So, he approached a sheep that was feeding its young and brought the little lion to it. The lion, smelling the warm milk and desperately hungry, clung to the ewe and fed on it. He did so for many days until he wanted to be weaned himself.

But what truly surprised the shepherd was that the lion eventually began to eat grass like sheep. Because he walked around with them all day and fed on grass, he began to think that he too was a sheep. He would walk wherever the sheep went and run with them to where the shepherd was when they saw a wolf or some other predator. The funny thing was that the lion was a very big animal, much bigger than a wolf but as he saw that the sheep were scared and ran trying to save their lives, he did the same. That's how he lived for some years, always scared and with a sheep mentality.

One day, while they were drinking water in the river, a hungry lion came out of the bushes and when he saw the group of sheep, he attacked them and with a single bite attacked the neck of one of them to kill it and eat it.

The lion who thought he was a sheep was nearby and watched what was happening. He lunged at the killer lion and fought him while all the sheep ran away, frightened. Suddenly, the aggressor lion preyed on him:

" Why are you attacking me? You are also a lion and we could share the prey."

The lion replied:

"I attack you because you killed one of my sisters."

"They are not your sisters! You are a lion."

"Of course not, I am a sheep, and that herd of sheep is my family."

"My friend, come with me." He took him to the river and said, "Look at yourself in the water, you are a lion."

When the lion-sheep looked at himself in the water and saw his resemblance to the aggressor lion, he realized that he was telling the truth.

"It's true," he said, confused. "But I can't leave the sheep. They took care of me and are like family to me."

"My friend, think, do you really want to live in fear all your life? Do you want to run away from wolves, foxes, and any other animal that threatens the sheep? Think that you have the ability to hunt and not be hunted, that you were born to frighten and not be frightened. Leave that life, return to your origins and become the powerful lion that you are."

"But they are my family and I can't abandon them now. They did everything for me and it's not fair for me to turn my back on them right now."

"Think, if you truly want to help them, start by realizing who you are. You have to get out of that sheep mentality because one sheep cannot help another sheep."

So the lion-sheep decided to accompany him to learn to live like a lion, and in that way, he no longer lived in fear of anything because he decided to be a hunter and not the victim and he began to live the lifestyle of a lion, to live the lifestyle he was born to live.

Like this lion, dear friend, many people do not dare to change because according to them, they cannot abandon the teachings that their parents gave them but in most cases, these parents live in poverty and sickness. They want their children to be just like them because they do not know anything different.

But you should know that our parents had their time and their moment and if they did not take advantage of it, it was their decision. But now, you have the opportunity to find your true identity, to discover that

LIFE LEAKAGES

you were born to be a hunter and not the prey, that you were not born to be afraid but to have courage and to defend your own because inside you is found the greatness and the capacity of your Creator.

And just as it happened to Tarzan or the lion, we know very well that this is inevitable. Your lifestyle will depend on the environment in which you grow up. That is why I invite you to look with love and respect at the people you grew up with: your parents, siblings, aunts, uncles, grandparents, and great-great-grandparents. See what they have accomplished. For example, how many of them finished college, how many of them had a career, and what was their lifestyle. If you don't like what you see in them, you will have to make changes because you may be imitating them and heading for a similar fate without even realizing it.

But today, you can decide to be yourself again. Don't be satisfied with just looking like you are doing a little better than the rest of your family, dare to believe that you are capable of showing everyone around you that you can be someone completely different, that you have the ability to think differently and not do what the rest of your family does, no matter what they think or say you should do.

LIFE LEAKAGES

Chapter 12
WE ARE ALL BORN WITH A MISSION IN LIFE

In Genesis 1:26, we read that when God set out to create man, he decided to make him in his image and likeness. This means that he created us in a way very similar to his own.

Now, I am sure that no matter what you believe in, what doctrine or religion you practice, if you read the Bible or have ever been to a mass, church, parish, or religious center, you surely know that God created heaven, earth, and all things that exist by simply saying and declaring it. Just by speaking and saying: let there be light, the light was made. Then he said: let there be the moon, and the sea, and the fish, and the wild beasts of the field, and all things, and all things were made.

I am sure that, if indeed you know this, you are convinced that what exists are great things but we have to be aware that everything was created with the thought of God and that when he began to speak about what he thought, things began to take shape.

And if we were made in the image and likeness of God and God made the world by thinking and speaking, then we can be sure that we too possess this ability to be able to create things in our thoughts, and begin to speak of them with the certainty that they will happen, and then watch everything around us make sense.

You just have to be convinced that He who created you and breathed life into you, also gave you the ability to create your own destiny and your own creations. That is why it is so important that you remove all negative words from your mouth and start speaking good things about yourself. Don't say that you can't; If you are facing a problem, such as an illness or a debt or a marital problem, instead of saying: "I can't take it anymore, I might as well resign myself to this misery" say: "I can handle this, and even though things don't look the way I want them to now, I know I wasn't born to live this way."

Don't condemn your life to misery by thinking and saying: "I'll never beat this problem."

The Book of Isaiah 40:31 says: "Those who hope in the Lord will renew their strength. They will soar on wings like eagles." Do you see? Inside you there is an extra-strength that you are not yet using because you were never told the truth about your Creator, you were never told the truth about who you were born to be. On the contrary, you were given very distorted information about who you are, but I am here and I bring you this written message from your Creator. He tells you not to throw in the towel, not to give up, and not to resign yourself to living in mediocrity.

You can do much more and if you see many problems around you, remember that you can triumph over them because you have wings like eagles. If you know a little about eagles, you will know that they use the force of the wind going with them to reach heights faster. In the same way, you can do it: The more trouble you have now, the more likely you are to soar like an eagle. Just look inside you, somewhere in your heart are those

LIFE LEAKAGES

strengths and divinity that your Creator put in you, and even if you don't see it, just believe it. Never again speak ill of yourself, but on the contrary, close your eyes and declare with audible words and with all your heart:

• •
"I was born to create and not to destroy. I was put here because I have a mission to improve my life and the lives of my loved ones. I will no longer declare defeat over my life, but I will believe and declare that all things that I can imagine and believe I can accomplish."
• •

I am sure that life will start to turn in your favor, just believe that there are already good things waiting for you and that's why you don't have to be envious of anything to anyone. Someone else's success is not your success, but your success will not be taken away by anyone but you.

So walk through life trusting that what is for you, no one is going to take it away from you. Start believing that there are great things out there waiting for you: that house, that car, that partner, maybe those clients for your business. Everything is out there and it belongs to you. What you have to do is change the negative thoughts and start having thoughts of triumph and victory. Even if you are sick, think that your healing is on its way; that you were born to be the voice of God on earth and the voice of God has authority.

Like Tarzan, you don't have to settle for living in a gorilla environment, or like a scared lion with a sheep mentality. If you continue to believe and live as someone you are not, you are not living your life, but the life someone else told you to live. This would be a life leakage, so do not live with fears, or bad thoughts of defeat or failure, rather think that you are more than that. Inside you, there is the greatness of your Creator, who made you with all the capabilities you need.

12.1 Deepening negative thoughts

During my life, I have met a lot of people with different thoughts and since I like learning a lot, I like to listen to everyone as much as possible. Thanks to this, I have learned that the only difference between a person who lives a happy and fulfilled life and one who is always dissatisfied is only his or her way of thinking.

For example, there are things we can avoid and there are things we can't: birds flying over your head is unavoidable, and nesting on your head is avoidable.

Likewise, bad, negative thoughts may be inevitable, but putting them into practice or accepting them in your mind as a reality can be avoided; growing older and aging on the outside is inevitable but aging on the inside is optional.

So the problem of failure in someone's life is by adopting thoughts of defeat and misery.

****
Our mind is like a magnet that attracts whatever we think about. If we think only of failing, failure will come to us. But, if we put an effort to have only thoughts of triumph and success, then triumph and success will come to us.
****

When a person has a life leakage and does not realize it, he loses the sense of being alive. That is why in these times, we look at little, old people of fifteen, twenty, or maybe forty years old. The truth is that there are people of many ages, and I say little, old people because these people, despite their age, have already grown old.

LIFE LEAKAGES

To explain it better, I encourage you to look at what is happening in the world today. You will realize that there are young people fifteen or twenty years old taking their own lives because they no longer have any sense of their existence and believe that death is better. Or we see elderly men, in their thirties, begging for money on the streets because they think they no longer have the time or the strength to get a good job. In their mind they are finished, they are old people who are waiting for death and can no longer start something new and ask for money to eat while they die.

But all that is only in their mind. It was there they lost the battle and let themselves be defeated by the negative thoughts that drained their life. They no longer live according to their years, but according to their defeat.

On the other hand, we look at 'young' people in their sixties and seventies. They are adults who look like old people but have never aged on the inside. Nothing ever got the better of them, they have a great sense of humor and in some cases, they are very active people who have to do something all the time. In fact, their mentality is that as long as they have life, they will decide how to live it and not the circumstances.

> *I have learned that the only difference between a person who lives a happy and fulfilled life and one who is always unhappy is only their way of thinking.*

It is important to note that in the end, it does not matter how we look on the outside, but how we are on the inside. Take good care of your mind so that your life does not escape and do not lose faith or the strength to always expect to do something new because the day you stop attempting to learn, you will stop living.

Remember that on the outside there will be thousands of reasons to become bitter and lose the course of your life. You cannot avoid them, but what you can avoid is letting them enter your mind.

The mind is like a ship sailing on the high seas. No matter how threatening the waves are and how violent the sea gets, as long as the water does not enter the ship, the ship will stay afloat and will not sink. In the same way, no matter what bad news or threats you hear around you every day, don't let them enter your mind so they cannot hurt you. Rather look at the positive things, take advantage of all your possibilities, and if you think you don't have any, build one yourself. After all, you have the quality to create things as your creator did, remember?

In 2008, the United States suffered a terrible financial crisis. Businesses closed their doors, jobs became scarce, shopping malls closed, and many lost their jobs and even their homes. I saw entire families sleeping under bridges, which was very sad because there were very young children and it was very cold.

The day you stop trying and learning, you will stop living.

All the people were very scared. My wife, my two children, and I lived in a very, very small apartment, and we were expecting a third child. I had also lost my job and we had already run out of savings; our bank accounts were at zero. People were on the streets begging for money and looking for work but, as I told you, there was none. The situation was so bad that many decided to emigrate to their countries of origin and some to other countries, but it was precisely in those days that life taught me what I have been telling you.

LIFE LEAKAGES

I knew that inside me was what I needed, that I had been created with all the qualities to use in any situation. So, when we thought we were ready to leave the small apartment and move to the nearest bridge with our two children and one on the way, my wife and I sat down, and after talking and crying for a long time, I said to her what I ask you to do, dear reader.

I said: "Jazmín, neither you nor I were born for this. This is not going to end with us, we will get out of this. I know very well that inside us there is such a creative idea that despite the crisis, we can carry it out. I am sure that God knew that we could go through these things, and surely he did not forget to put in us what we needed to face this journey in our lives."

And although we had hundreds of reasons to complain, we decided to get up, stop crying, and stop lamenting. We began to think about what we knew how to do and what resources we had. Jazmín told me that since she was a little girl she helped her mother make tortillas, and they were very tasty, and I was a witness to that.

When she said that, our eyes lit up because the idea came to us at the same time. We thought that despite the crisis, people would still have to eat, and consequently, they would take care getting the money to buy tortillas, so if we offered them warm homemade tortillas, they would surely buy from us.

It was then that we stood up, hugged each other, laughed, and this time we cried, but no longer out of worry, but out of happiness, thanking God that we did not let ourselves be dragged down by our circumstances, but to stand by what we believed in.

That same afternoon, Jazmín taught me how to make the tortillas. We used the only two small bags of corn flour we had and began making the homemade tortillas. That same night I went out knocking on different doors of houses and apartments and offered the best tortillas in the neighborhood. Some said no, but some said yes, and I began to sell the tortillas and bring some money into the house.

Later, after I had learned to make the tortillas, we increased the production. We turned that small apartment into a mini-factory of homemade tortillas. Every day we sold more and more, and every time the customers asked me for more, so much so that I had to say that we could no longer sell to new customers because, as I told you, the apartment where we lived was too small; besides, Jazmín was about to give birth to our third child.

To finish this story, I would like to tell you that now I no longer sell tortillas but I learned a great lesson: That no crisis can stop us, that circumstances do not decide how we are going to live, but only we do.

It was from that experience that something came out that was already inside me and I did not know it. That is why, dear reader, I encourage you not to let bad circumstances limit you or attempt to break you. You are a winner and not a failure. I don't know what you are going through right now but I know that you will get through it and that it will happen to you just like it did to me, that when the crisis ended, with it ended my excuses and my limitations.

I saw clearly how that bad experience only made me and my family stronger. It was in a time of crisis when my mentality changed and since then I have learned

LIFE LEAKAGES

from business. I knew that there was more than just selling my life and exchanging it for money.

I understood that sometimes it is not money what we need, but believing that we have everything we need. Encourage yourself to have thoughts of abundance and not scarcity, invest and try taking risks, after all, life is about risks and learning.

There is no crisis that can stop us because circumstances do not decide how we are going to live, but ourselves.

LIFE LEAKAGES

Chapter 13
BAD HABITS

Bad habits are terrible enemies for someone who wants to live a full life without wasting time. In fact, there are habits of death: They are the habits you have, even though you know they harm your health or make you or your family suffer.

Although there are many bad habits, here I want to talk to you about one that, if you are imprisoned by it, it is surely making your life and you do not realize it.

This bad habit is about your finances and consists of spending more than you earn. People who practice this bad habit are usually those who always intend to buy something even though they do not have enough money and think that they must have everything that is coming out in the market, and they end up in debt. There are thousands of people who live waiting for their paycheck to survive; they usually get their paycheck on a Friday and Tuesday they are at zero again. They are the ones who always blame the government for the misery in which they live or think that everyone else is to blame for not having enough money but, in truth, everything that happens to them is due to the bad habit of spending more than they earn.

Maybe I am writing something that may sound very rude, but if you take a good look or if you were to visit someone today who has financial problems and is almost always borrowing money, you would realize that he has the biggest and most expensive TV on the market, he will have many video games and things they offer on TV, good and expensive things that should not be within his reach, but he still has them.

Now, if these things are never needed to live, why do so many people even get credit to buy them? Because they are imprisoned in the bad habit of spending and marketing take advantage of that to sell them their products. If you are wondering what this has to do with the journey of life, I will answer that, as I told you before, the system we live in buys our time with money. You normally leave your family every day because you have to be present at your job; otherwise, you wouldn't get paid. In other words, what you are selling is your time, and when you sell your time, you are selling your life. Now, do you understand?

Therefore, if you pay attention to this habit, you will realize that every time you are going to pay for some product or service received, you are paying with part of your life because it was in exchange for your life that you got that money, and if you look at it from this point of view, you will realize that you are buying many things that do not deserve to be paid with your life.

••••••••••••••••••••••••••••••••••••
That is why it is so important not to waste your money on things that are not worth it because having the habit of misspending your money is like wasting your life.
••••••••••••••••••••••••••••••••••••

This habit is a killer that kills your most valuable resource: your time and the number of days you were given.

Right now, I encourage you to think if there are things you spend your money on that you don't truly need because the fewer payments you have, the less

LIFE LEAKAGES

you will have to work, and if you work less, you will save time. Time is life, so take care of it and invest it in the things you truly like to do. Get out of the bad habit of spending too much, and discipline yourself. If possible, take a course on how to manage your finances and you will see how your lifestyle will change and you will live freely and efficiently.

13.1 The time of life is like a bank account

Job 14:5 says, "A man's days are numbered. He cannot live longer than the time You have set."

Taking these words into account we can say what we already know, that one day we are going to die and that is why we are sure that we only have a certain number of days unknown to us, and that daily we use that lifespan.

To understand better, let's say that a person who loves you leaves you an inheritance of eighty thousand dollars in the currency of your country. The person who gave you that amount will not be able to give you more, now it depends on you to know how to manage this inheritance well, not only to keep it but to multiply it and pass it on to your children who will come after you.

You will have two options: waste that inheritance, which is what most people do, or use it to multiply it, and leaves not eighty thousand to your children, but much more.

I hope I don't mess you up with these numbers, but I tell you this so you know that just as it happens with a bank account, also in the account of the days you will live, you will have to decide if you spend your life wasting it on meaningless things and bad habits that the world can offer you, or if you decide to work with it and manage it well to leave a good legacy to your children after you.

If you decide to free yourself and teach your children not to fall prey to bad habits, they will have your example and your legacy, and they will surely be better and go further because they did not waste their time in the prisons of these habits that are undoubtedly a life leakage.

13.2 Toxic relationships

Although love relationships can lead us to experience things and pleasures so nice and beautiful that they are often difficult to forget, they can also be leaks of life.

I have heard the saying: "How nice it is to love and be loved back." And that is very true: however, we cannot ignore that there are very harmful and toxic friendships or love relationships.

Let's look at it this way: When a person is single, they are free to come and go wherever they want. They can visit their parents and friends, spend as much time as they want with them, and spend as much time as required with a friendship or a family relationship. When they find a partner, they expect that it will add more value to their life, that if they were happy until then, now that happiness will multiply because they have someone to share it with. Or at least that is how it should be.

However, when an individual enters into a relationship and instead of their life having more value, they find that it is meaningless because of their partner's demands and jealousy, we can say that it is a toxic relationship.

LIFE LEAKAGES

13.3 The relationship in marriage

Sometimes we feel that marriage is a never-ending problem, but we must remember that it is not our thoughts that define what a marriage relationship should be like, but that the institution of marriage is already outlined by its inventor, who is God.

Until a married couple comes to know its principles and importance, they feel blessed and fortunate to be married.

Perhaps you have heard many times that marriage is very difficult and that it is mostly pure suffering, but if we stop to look at the people who hold that opinion, we realize that they are people who have not yet understood or learned the principles of marriage. They have come to believe that marriage is a partnership of two people to satiate each other's sexual desire.

In fact, we can say that when a couple has that concept of their marriage, it is very obvious that they look at their partner as an object who is obligated to give them pleasure as many times as they want for everything to work. Living a marriage on such principles is terrible because the one who demands from his spouse to fulfill all the obligations of marriage without giving anything in return will never be satiated. And the other person will be the victim of this association.

Another fact that hurts a couple a lot is when they think that marriage is about fulfilling household chores. For example, when the man thinks that his wife, because she is the woman, has to do all the household chores and take care and educate the children on her own, not to mention that he may believe that she is the one who has to make the effort to keep him sexually satisfied.

A woman in these circumstances is not living her life, but that of her husband. And no one deserves to come into this world and leave it without having lived.

> *And no one deserves to come into this world and leave it without having lived.*

This happens in many homes because of the culture in which we grow up, depending on our society.

In many families, it is the mothers who are in charge of raising their children, and unfortunately, when these children grow up and get married, they have the mentality that it is the women who must do everything for them and that they are not there to serve anyone.

This problem also exists when the wife thinks that the man is a work machine and that he must work to have enough money to satisfy all their desires and that if he does not, he will be a bad husband.

In the case of many women, they believe that when they get married things will continue to be the same as when they were with their parents, who indulged them and ended up fulfilling all their desires.

If you are reading this and you are single, let me give you some good advice to get a good partner to share your life with. You have to observe very well before starting a romantic relationship with someone, and here is a key point.

First, get to know the candidate in their relationship with their parents. If they have a good relationship with them, then they will be a very good person to start a relationship with. Many young people start a relationship without thinking that they may end up in love and married to someone who does not respect their parents.

You may wonder what a parent-child relationship has to do with a couple. Well, when a young person can't respect those who brought them to life, taught them to go to the bathroom, bathe and eat by themselves, spent time on their homework, fed them, and gave them food, shelter, clothes, and love, they won't respect you either.

If they are ungrateful to the people who love them most, certainly, they will also be ungrateful to you. If they betray and lie to their parents, who gave them everything, how can they not lie to you, who they don't even know well?

If you are reading this book and you have children, you must discuss these things with them so that they know how to choose the person with whom they will share their lives.

LIFE LEAKAGES

Chapter 14
MARRIAGE AND ITS CONCEPT

We need to know that marriage is the most serious and important association on earth. In fact, we can say that cities and nations are made up of families, but the foundation of a good or bad family is marriage.

The local government of your city wants to have control and order of the entire city, that is, no violence, no robberies, and no other type of crime. To achieve this they have created institutions and programs to help parents educate their children but by this time, we should have realized that some things are not working because crime continues to increase and violence is the order of the day. But nobody gives importance to marriages. In other words, we want good young people but we don't take care of the most important foundation: a good marriage.

Many of our young people grow up without a father or a mother because mom and dad did not know how to handle a relationship in peace and chose the easy way, which was a separation that teaches their children that the easiest way is to run away from problems. What do you think these abandoned children are going to do when they get married and face a marital problem? That's right, you guessed it! They will run away from the problem and leave other abandoned children behind as they go in search of new adventures. They don't know that they haven't truly abandoned the problem because the problem has been with them since they learned it as children.

If we go deeper into this subject, we will realize that all this happens because we forget the importance of this institution. As a minister, I have married many couples but beforehand, in a few talks, I teach them about the commitment they are about to undertake. After letting them know their responsibilities, I can see in their eyes how scared they become because, until that day, they had only thought about the party, the white dress, and above all, the honeymoon. Then, they look at each other as if to say, "We still have time." Or maybe they think: "Why did we choose this guy to marry us?"

I don't know if you are married or not, or if you say: "I am in free union" but if you are living with someone and have sexual relations, the rules of marriage are for you. Here I will show you some things that you give when you get married and that, if you follow them to the letter, I assure you that they will become a guarantee for your happiness in your life and your relationship.

First, you should know that when a person decides to unite their life with someone else, at that moment a contract of association is made with the person they love.

That is why you must be very careful with whom you are going to share your life. Remember, the most valuable and beautiful thing you have is the time you spend on this planet and it would truly be a shame to waste it with someone who does not even know if they are alive.

LIFE LEAKAGES

Remember, before you decide to unite your life with someone else, you must be sure if they are the one you truly need by your side. Because, just like the children's story of Little Red Riding Hood and the Big Bad Wolf, you can also be surrounded by wolves who are disguised as nobility and love, but who will eventually bring out their true nature and ruin your life.

Let's imagine that two people want to start a business together and work as partners. They will both feel that they have the same rights because they each made an investment, and they will be working in the same business; therefore, they will want to receive benefits and profits so they can earn a very good lifestyle.

To be honest, they both have the right to reap the fruits of all their effort and work because they invested the same amount of money and worked the same amount of time. It's also only fair that they should have the same earnings, right? But what if you start making less, what if you start believing that you need more? They will probably split up, go out of business, and leave thinking they are victims of their former partner.

The most valuable and beautiful thing you have is the time of your stay on this planet and it would be a real shame if you were to waste it on someone who doesn't even know if he is alive.

And if one of them came to you and told you the problem, surely you would say that if the investment was the same on both sides and the work was the same for both of them, it would be fair for the profits to be shared equally, right?

Well, with this example, we can plainly see the association with marriage. You should know very well that, by doing this, you are both committing to make the same investment; therefore, you are both entitled to receive the benefits of the marriage.

In my profession as a minister, I have met many couples who do not understand this, and one always demands more than one is given, which causes many problems in the institution of marriage. When one of the two feels that they deserve more and begins to demand more, the relationship can become toxic, especially for the one who receives the demands.

This happens because many people think they can reap something without having sown, but we must understand that no one can give what he or she does not have. If you want to feel loved, you must first love. You must give what you want to receive.

As I told you, I grew up in the fields. I always watched the sowing and the reaping, and I grew up very convinced that no one will reap what he did not sow and that each one reaps what he sows.

No one can give what they do not have and this is very simple and easy to understand: if you want to feel loved, first you have to love, you will have to give love if what you want to receive is love.

In the fields, it is of utmost importance to know the planting seasons. You cannot afford to do it only when it suits you, but only when the weather allows it. Despite that, I remember watching many people during my childhood who, out of laziness, did not take advantage of the planting season and just slept or rested.

LIFE LEAKAGES

Those of us who sowed and worked without rest received a good and abundant harvest, but when we went home to enjoy what we sowed one day, lazy people would appear at our door and beg for mercy, asking for a little portion of the harvest, promising that they would pay us back later.

Perhaps the comparison seems a bit old-fashioned to you, but this is also the way it happens in couples. No one wants to show affection, love, time, and effort to make their spouse feel happy, but then the spouse spends their time complaining and asking those who do sow these good things in their marriages how they do it so well and asks for help to improve their relationship.

If you dare to sow good things in the person with whom you share your life, you will reap and gather what you sow, but if you do not sow anything due to laziness, do not expect to receive anything because anyone who gives nothing has no right to ask or expect anything at all, except what they can get from the mercy of others.

A bad marital relationship can be fatal for someone who intends to their live to the fullest. There is nothing more regrettable than falling into the mistake of living trying to please someone who does not value anything you do, and the worst thing is that despite giving your best, you still have to beg for love, attention, and understanding. Friend, I hope this is not your case, but you have to be aware that you were not born to live someone else's life, but to live your own life. I have seen many unhappy people living a miserable life, men, and women who beg love from their partners every day, and although their spouses have been unfaithful to them on different occasions, they are clinging to be with them. They believe that they will not be able to rebuild their lives if they stay alone, but that is not true. What happens is that even in misery our body and mind get used to it.

> *Anyone who gives nothing has no right to ask or expect anything at all.*

Just like a bird that was created to fly but is born in captivity and does not know its capabilities, so too our mind can be held captive in such a way that we may be suffering and not realize it.

That is why I ask you with much love and respect, whomever you are and wherever you are, that you dare to live your life and get away from all those who prevent you from doing so. You were not born to be anyone's slave, but to be free and happy. Take advantage of the time you still have left and dare to live without fear, stay away from people who do not add value to your life and relate to people who think well of you, surround yourself with people who can see your value and help you to be a better person.

LIFE LEAKAGES

Chapter 15
SEBASTIAN'S STORY

To help you better understand all these issues of utmost importance for your life, I will tell you a story that, although it is a bit long, I can assure you that will be a very helpful conclusion to understand more of what we have learned so far.

Surely you have heard the story of a boy who felt he was worthless. He was a young man who was surrounded by people but still felt like crap. He was so frustrated that he felt he never did anything right and one day he decided to end his miserable life.

So he thought: "Before I take my life, I will go to the old man who they say is very wise and who lives on the outskirts of town to tell him of my misfortune. If he does not have good advice for me or a good reason for me not to take my life, then I will end this misery today."

So he walked to the wise man's house and when he arrived, he announced his arrival by shouting and waving:

"Hello! Hello! Is anyone here? Hello?"

Suddenly he heard and sensed someone approaching behind him. Startled, he turned and saw the old man approaching with a pile of freshly hewn firewood on his shoulder. In a slightly tired voice, he asked the boy:

"What do you want? Why did you come here? Nobody ever comes here. What do you need? Tell me quickly and get out of here!"

"Hello, sir. My name is Sebastian and I came here because I'm tired of living. Lately, I've been feeling a lot of pressure because everyone demands something from me, and even though I try my best and do my best, it's never enough. In fact, everyone tells me I'm a fool and that's never going to change. So, I thought I would come and tell you my misfortune and see if you can give me some advice that will convince me not to take my life. If you have nothing for me, then I will end this misery today."

While the boy was telling these things to the wise old man, he was taking the wood down from his shoulder and lighting a small fire, heating a delicious coffee in a very old, rustic-looking metal pot from which a very rich aroma was coming out. The smoke from the burning wood would rise and paint a column of grey between the small house and the clouds.

"I see that your situation is not at all easy," replied the wise old man, "but since you are determined to take your own life, I would like to ask you to do me a great favor."

"A favor? I came here to get some advice and maybe some help, and you're asking me for a favor?"

"Yes, my boy, if you think that this afternoon you are going to die, at least you could do something good by helping this poor old man."

As the wise man continued talking, Sebastian thought: "This man is crazy, I don't even think he understood my problem, but maybe he is right. Before I end my life I could help him and I will leave with the satisfaction that at least I did something good."

LIFE LEAKAGES

And in a somewhat annoyed voice, he said: "Well, tell me what you need."

"You see," replied the wise old man, "I've needed to sell this ring for a long time." He reached into his old leather satchel slung over his left shoulder and pulled out a beautiful ring that glittered in the sunlight. "It was my wife's. I gave it to her when she married me, but one day she got sick and died, and since then I have kept this jewel, but now I am old and I have decided to sell it to survive."

"Where do you want me to sell it and how many coins do I ask for?"

"Well, first I want you to know that it's very valuable to me and I don't want you to sell it to a jewelry store or a merchant because they will only look at it as a business and profit from it. That's why I'm asking you to sell it to a person you trust and who you are sure will keep it. You will only sell it for two coins."

"Only two coins?" Sebastian asked. "I think it's too little, but anyway, it's your ring, and it will be the last thing I do. I'll sell it, bring you the coins and then I'll take my life."

Sebastian snatched the ring from the wise man's hands, put it in his trouser pocket, and walked back to the village where he lived to sell it.

When he got to town, he immediately went to the square, and began to offer the ring. He showed it to as many people as he could, but to no avail. People looked at the ring and said: "I don't think it has value," "I don't think it's worth the two coins," "I don't think it's pure gold." In the end, the ring could not be sold.

Before returning to the old man's house, he thought, "I can see that this old man needs the coins and I am about to die, so I will make one last effort," and he began to knock on all the doors. When they opened their door, he offered them that beautiful ring. He told them that a crazy old fool only wanted two coins for it. But people would say to him the same words as those in the square: "I don't think this ring is worth two coins."

Others said that perhaps the ring was made of some worthless material, and only a few people offered one coin, but the young man said he could not accept because the owner wanted two. When he had finished going through all the streets and houses, he decided to return to the old man.

As he walked, he regretted not having taken his own life sooner because, after all, what was he alive for if he was worthless to anyone? He thought that, since he was a child, his parents had wanted him to be like his brothers, and since he never could be, they always said he was a pain in the ass. His parents fought a lot and, one day, his dad stormed out of the house yelling and saying very rude things, his mom said he left because he made them fight a lot. At his school, he was never able to be someone his parents or anyone else could be proud of. He never got a visit from his parents at his school and at important events, they never showed up. This had been very painful because he watched as his classmates' parents came, hugged them, brought them food to class, sometimes even carried them. He thought how lucky they were to have parents like that.

He remembered that one day he decided to arrive early before the school opened and all his classmates and teachers arrived. He had waited at the front door, and when the teachers arrived he said to them:

"Teachers, what a pity you didn't arrive earlier today."

"Why, Sebastian?" They asked him.

"Because today my parents came to drop me off at school."

LIFE LEAKAGES

"Really? That's good! Congratulations, we are very pleased!"

"Yes, me too, thank you for congratulating me."

When his classmates arrived, he told them the same story and some of them rejoiced. Although deep in his heart he knew it was a total lie, he liked to believe that his parents spent time with him.

He remembered that when he left home, he thought it would solve things for both his family and himself. But that had caused more wounds in his heart because he had to learn to live on the street, to go hungry, and learn to survive even though he was just a child. At night, to protect himself from the cold, he had to sleep among pigs and horses on a small farm. A couple of days later, the owners took notice and gave him a job cleaning the excrement from the pens, so he was able to get food.

When he heard that his parents were desperately looking for him, he was overjoyed because he thought they had finally realized that he was important to their lives and he returned. But when he arrived, he was scolded because, although they were worried, they got mad that the neighbors were talking about him leaving home. At that moment, the boy resigned himself to the fact that he would never be loved and so he wanted to put an end to this life of bitterness.

And so Sebastian was lost in thought as he approached the sage's house. As he crossed a small stream, a soft breeze touched his face and he remembered that in that very place he had gone for a walk with a pretty girl.

He slowed down the pace and speed of his steps and thought:

"How could I think a girl like her would notice me? After all, no one ever liked me. I should have realized it before she betrayed me and left me for that popular boy?"

»"What makes me most angry is that the day I went to see her, I found her talking to him. I remember we were only seventeen, but I thought we were going to get married. That day she said she would decide on one of us, and for a moment I thought she would choose me, but how wrong I was! For they both looked me in the eye, and she opened her mouth to tell me she preferred him. I could not restrain myself, and before tears came out of my eyes, I went away to hide and cry alone."

And so, without realizing it, our friend Sebastian arrived at the wise man's house, who had a delicious meal prepared on a grill. By the smell, Sebastian knew it was roast lamb. Next to it was some bread and a pitcher of freshwater.

"I see you're back," said the old man, "and just in time to eat."

He took a plate made of solid clay, put almost half a rack of lamb and a piece of bread on it, and gave it to Sebastian.

"Eat, my good friend. I imagine you are hungry."

"Thank you very much, sir. Truth is, I feel like I'm fainting from hunger."

Sebastian sat down and ate desperately. When he was almost finished, the wise man said:

"By the look in your eyes, I see that you have been crying. Why? Didn't you sell the ring?"

"I'm sorry, it's true, sir. I could not sell the ring, so I am returning it to you."

"But you must not cry over this," said the man as he took the ring in his hands.

"That's not why I was crying, sir."

"Oh, it isn't? Why then?"

LIFE LEAKAGES

Sebastian took a glass, poured himself some water, and drank, looking at the sky. Then, he put the glass down, looked at the ground, and began to explain:

"Listen, my life has not been easy at all, I don't know if it's my fault or the fault of others. I cried because I remembered my childhood and the love I needed so much and never felt. As you should know, when you are a child, you are not interested in riches or anything that has to do with material things, you only want to be loved and admired by the people you love. If these things were lacking, then everything would be lacking. And that happened to me in my childhood."

"Don't feel that way, Sebastian. After all, people sometimes don't know how to love because they too were never loved, but I'm sure that one day someone will come into your life who will love you just the way you are."

"I thought the same thing for a while, sir. One day, I gave my love and my heart to a beautiful young woman, but I think this caused me more wounds than I already had and that is why I believe that people cannot love if they do not perceive that they are going to receive something in return. And as you see, I have nothing to give, I never have, so I always begged for love in many ways. I even lied and made up stories to my classmates when I was a child telling them that my parents took me to school and that my mother even made food for me to take to school so I wouldn't go hungry."

"Don't think like that, Sebastian. What's happening is that you haven't known true love, but that doesn't mean it doesn't exist. True love doesn't ask for anything in return, nor does it expect to be reciprocated. It just loves, and you have had to beg for love, as you say, because you think you have to pay for that love and you have nothing to offer. But if you want someone to love you without any interest, you must first know who you are so that others can see it. If you don't value yourself, how will anyone else be able to see the value in you? Besides, it's not bad that you feel an emptiness now because, after all, people were made to be loved. But if you allow yourself to believe and let true love be..."

"Excuse the interruption, sir, but I don't believe or want any of that anymore! Besides, I didn't come here so you could send me to sell a ring. But now I've already returned it to you and I thank you for the food."

Sebastian stood up, took the rope he had been holding from the beginning, and tried to say goodbye.

"Oh, that's right, I forgot that you had a date with your death. But how come you're leaving like this, boy, if you haven't sold my ring?"

"I told you I tried everything, but nobody wants to pay two coins for your ring! And now, if I may, I have something more important to do and I feel I've already wasted a lot of time with you!"

"All right, but just think, if you take your life now, you'll leave this poor old man without two coins and I'll die too. Besides, the sun is still in the middle of the sky, you still have plenty of time to go again and sell this ring."

• •
*True love does not ask for anything in return,
nor does it expect to be reciprocated. It just loves.*
• •

"I already told you that nobody wants to buy it! Why don't you understand?! Besides, who else am I going to offer it to if I've already shown it to everyone in the village?!"

The wise old man looked into Sebastian's eyes and put his hand on the boy's arm and said to him:

LIFE LEAKAGES

"Please go for a last time to the village to sell this ring, but do not offer it to the people, offer it to the jewelers and merchants. And now, boy, no matter how much they offer you, I ask you to show it, but not to sell it. If you do this for me, I will help you accomplish what you want to do when you return. Do we have a deal?"

Sebastian thought about it for a moment and then nodded.

"All right, sir, but I want you to know very well that this is all a wast e of time. And I don't understand why are you asking me to sell the ring but at the same time not to sell it."

"Ah, but you have nothing to lose. Just think that if you're willing to take your own life, which is not understandable, why wouldn't you do something like what I'm asking you to do?"

While the wise man was still talking, Sebastian thought:

'This old man is crazy and very stubborn. I think that if I don't do what he asks me to do, I won't be able to die in peace. I'll go to a couple of jewelry stores and after offering them this ring, I'll come back, throw it at him, and go die in peace.'

"All right, sir, don't tell me anymore! Give me that ring, I want to get out of here!"

"Very good decision, boy, I thank you for doing this for me. But remember, no matter how many coins they offer you, don't sell this ring. I want you to bring it with you when you return."

"Yes, I got it! I'm leaving now, sir." As he walked away, Sebastian said: "I want you to know that this is the last favor I am doing for you, and also that I am disappointed in you because I came here looking for possible help and I got the opposite. But anyway, I will go and do as you ask and I won't be very long!"

And so, as he walked away, Sebastian's voice was lost.

-oOo-

15.1 Second attempt

The boy walked back to the village, that despite not being very big, the bustle of people never ended, there were always people selling or buying something.

While our friend Sebastian was walking, he arrived again at the small stream where he had remembered the girl who had broken his heart and it was inevitable for him not to think about it again.

In his mind, he began to say to himself: "Why did I have to live this life? Why have I never been able to do anything good? If only I was at least better looking or had a different appearance so I could feel good, then maybe I would meet a beautiful girl, get married, and have a family. Because what's the point of being alive, if I have to be alone? I imagine it must be a nice thing to know that someone cares about you, or that there's someone you can care about but if I couldn't get that with my parents or my brothers, how did I think I would get it with someone I don't even know?"

At that point, Sebastian looked at two very small bobcats that had gotten lost from their mother. One was trying to encourage the other to go under a small bush, where Sebastian assumed his home was located. It came to our friend's memory the names of his siblings, he sighed and wondered, "What has become of them?" Despite the quarrels and discord, he missed them and he said to himself:

LIFE LEAKAGES

"Maybe I was to blame for never getting along with them. I always felt that I was competing with some of them for my parent's attention and that I could never beat them. This provoked wounds within me that, to this day, have not been able to heal. For some time, I thought that they wished me ill, maybe because of all the blows I had received from some of them."

This was what he was thinking when he heard a voice shouting and saying:

"Hey, boy! Boy! Yeah, you, whoever you are, scare that sheep by the side of the road so it'll return to the others!"

It was a shepherd who was having difficulty keeping the sheep together.

"Which one, sir?"

"That one by the side of the road," answered the shepherd as he thought about how distracted Sebastian was.

"Oh, yes, I see it."

And he began to scare it back to its shepherd, but the little sheep resisted, so he approached it very slowly and softly stroked its ears; then Sebastian walked towards the shepherd, and little by little the sheep followed him. The shepherd was impressed and asked him:

"How did you do that, boy? How did you learn to make the sheep follow you?"

"Ah, it's not difficult, sir. Usually, these animals like to feel safe, and when they find safety in a person, they follow."

"I'm most impressed! What's your name, boy?"

"Sebastian, sir."

"Hello Sebastian, how do you do! My name is Anselmo. Tell me, where did you learn about sheep? Are you a shepherd too?"

"No, Mr. Anselmo, but some time ago, I took care of my father's sheep and those of some other villagers and farmers who paid me for it."

"So, you looked after a lot of them?"

"There weren't many but enough to keep me very busy and attentive all day."

"And what happened? You didn't like being a shepherd?"

"Well, you see, I was still very young when I did this work, and I don't know if I liked it or not, but it was a very difficult thing for me because I was always afraid of the ferocious animals that threaten to devour sheep."

And with a slightly mocking laugh, Anselmo said:

"Were you afraid that an animal would eat you too?"

"Yes. As you can see, I was very cowardly, but truly, more than the animals, I was afraid of my father because if I lost a sheep I would have to face him. Also, while the other children were playing in the street or outside their houses, I had to look after these animals. At times, they would get together and come to bother me and scare my flock, and while I was running after the sheep they would laugh at me a lot. This caused great wounds that somehow I think I still have not been able to overcome."

Anselmo, now in a more serious way, asked him:

"But why didn't you talk about this with your father or someone in your family so that they could help you?"

Sebastian lowered his gaze and with a broken voice continued:

"I tried many times, but nobody paid attention to me. At home everyone thought I was very stupid, my parents repeated that every time they could, and I think that's the main reason why they didn't pay attention to me. Sometimes they said that I only said that because I was lazy and didn't want to take care of sheep anymore. To not create more arguments, I just kept quiet and suffered in silence, longing with all my soul to grow up and escape from all that pain and the fears that are very difficult for a child to overcome."

Anselmo was very indignant and wanted to encourage Sebastian.

"Look, my boy, when a person becomes an adult, they become insensitive and forget that they were also a child and that they had fears. That's why it's hard for them to understand a child. Despite everything you tell me, are you still living at home?

"No, Anselmo, as soon as I could I ran away from everything and everyone."

"You mean you hate or came to hate your own family?"

At that moment, Sebastian lowered his gaze and, feeling uncomfortable with Anselmo's question, answered:

"Well, I think I have to go. It's late and I have an errand to run and then I have to take a trip from which there is no return. It was nice helping you and talking to you for a moment. Goodbye, my friend."

"Yes, goodbye, Sebastian. I hope your life is changing for the better. Cheer up, times are always changing and I believe the coming times will favor you."

And so, our friend Sebastian continued his short journey towards the town, which was already visible in the distance. The large, tall chimneys jutted out above all the houses, and the cross that stood atop a large chapel was the tallest of all the buildings. As he approached, the bells of a clock were heard throughout the town, announcing the change of the hour.

In the meantime, he thought about the talk he had with the sheepherder and felt anger. "At last, I will no longer live and I'll stop feeling this anger," he said to himself. "I wonder why. Why didn't I have a father to play with me? Why didn't I have a mother that would put me on her lap, hold me to her breast and tell me that she loved me?"

At that moment, two very thick tears came out of our friend's brown eyes, and he said in a firm but soft voice:

"Why is it that despite all my efforts I never received an 'I am proud of you!' How much I would give to hear from the mouth of one of my parents those words! But I am convinced that will never happen."

Suddenly, he realized that he was already in front of a small jewelry store, so he wiped his tears, sighed loudly and deeply, and went inside. A little discouraged, he greeted with a very shy voice:

"Good afternoon. Are you the one who is in charge of selling and buying the jewelry?"

"Of course I am, young man, come in! And tell me, what can I help you with? Do you want to buy something that catches your eye?"

"No. Well, yes. No, well, you see, sir, I have a ring and I'd like you to look at it and tell me if it's worth something and how many coins you could give me for it."

"Oh, I get it, kid, you're here as a salesman. That's all right. Show me that jewel, but I warn you that I am a very good merchant and you will not be able to take advantage of me."

As he spoke, Sebastian took out the ring and put it on the palm of his hand. When the jewelry expert looked at it, he opened his eyes wide and asked him in surprise:

LIFE LEAKAGES

"Where did you get this jewel, my boy?" He took out a small magnifying glass and looked at it very carefully, then said enthusiastically and almost shouting: "Tell me how many coins you want, and I'll give them to you!"

Sebastian was confused as to how a ring despised by many people who would not pay two coins for it now captured the interest of a jeweler, but he remembered that the wise old man had told him not to sell it no matter how many coins he was offered.

"No, sir, this ring is not for sale. Remember, I only said I wanted you to look at it and tell me if it was worth anything."

The jeweler looked him straight in the eye.

"Boy, please sell me this jewel! Look, if you want, I'll give you seventy-five coins right now."

Sebastian was even more surprised, but he said:

"No, sir, I cannot sell this ring."

He took it, started to leave, and when he was almost crossing the door that led to the street, the jeweler shouted at him:

"Boy, I'll give you a hundred coins! Please, sell it to me!"

But Sebastian left in a hurry and after walking for a while he stopped. He took the ring in his hands and wondered what was going on and how that rejected ring was worth so much.

"Maybe this jeweler is crazy and just wanted to play a joke on me. It would be good for me to go to the jewelry store next to the church and ask how much they would pay me if I sold it to them."

He walked to the next jewelry store. This one was a little bigger because it was next to the church. People used to shop there after mass, so when Sebastian arrived many people were looking and asking about the jewels that were on display. When he saw that one of the sales clerks was heading towards the inner part where the offices were located, he hurried and said:

"Excuse me! Excuse me! Sir!"

The man stopped.

"What do you want? We're very busy."

"I won't take up much of your time, I just came to show you a ring to ask you if it has any value and, if so, to tell me how much you would pay me for it."

He put the ring in the seller's hands, and when the seller looked at it, he said:

"Where on earth did you get this, boy? It's worth half the jewelry store! Come with me."

They went inside the shop, and the sales clerk took him to the owner of the jewelry store.

"Sir, I want you to take a look at this."

When the owner stood up and with a magnifying glass looked at the ring, he opened his eyes wide.

"But what is this?" He said in a low voice. Then he turned to Sebastian, who was even more surprised. "Boy, sell me this jewel, I'll give you two hundred coins for it.

Sebastian gulped.

"I can't, sir, I only came here to see how much this ring was worth, but I can't sell it to you."

"Then, if you change your mind, come here and I'll give you two hundred and thirty coins. I think that's a very good offer."

Sebastian took the ring and hurried out. "Why is this ring worth so much?" He asked himself, very confused, "How is it that someone who knows so much about jewelry wants to give me so much for it when at first glance it looks just like the others? I know I said I would only visit two jewelry stores, but just to be sure I'm not being pranked, I'll go to the one on the way out of town."

LIFE LEAKAGES

And he walked towards the exit of that beautiful town. When he finally arrived, he found the owner negotiating with a merchant who apparently was the supplier of gold and silver. To Sebastian, the owner sounded very greedy, and he thought, "This guy is only looking out for his own interests. Surely he wants to offer me a pittance for this ring, maybe only the two coins I originally asked for."

After the merchant left, he approached very timidly and said to the jeweler.

"Excuse me, sir?"

But he was looking at the merchandise he had just bought and without looking up, he answered him:

"What do you want, friend? Do you want to buy some jewelry? If not, I'm not interested in talking to you."

"Well, I wanted to ask if you could help me with your knowledge and tell me if this ring I have in my hands has a significant value and, if so, how many coins would you give me in exchange?

The jeweler was still looking at the merchandise.

"I am not interested in looking at your ring, and even if I were, I could not buy it from you because I have just spent all my money on this, which is of very good quality."

"Sir, I beg you, it is very important to me. Just look at it, give me your point of view and then I will leave you alone."

Very annoyed, the jeweler raised his head.

"I hope you keep your word and get out of here without delay. Let me see."

Sebastian put the ring in his hands. He looked at it and held his breath for a few seconds, then put it next to many other rings, and there Sebastian saw that although the workmanship of the ring was very similar to the others, next to hundreds of rings it had something that made it look very different.

"My friend, I have just spent all my coins on this bag of merchandise and I have no more to offer you, but I will give you all the silver and gold I have just bought in exchange for this ring."

Sebastian took the ring back.

"No, sir, I can't sell it."

Then the jeweler took some jewels out of his display cases and added them to the bag containing gold and silver.

"Boy, the bag has more value. Take it with you in exchange for that ring, it's a very good deal."

But Sebastian just thanked him and, very confused, walked down the main street of the town to return to the old man's house. As he walked, he felt his heart beating stronger and felt that life was teaching him something, but he could not perceive what it was. However, something inside him told him that a good change was waiting for him.

"I know, I'm going back to the old man. I'm sure he knows something about all this and that's why he asked me not to sell this ring. Of course, what a fool I am, he wants to teach me something with all this."

Thinking about that, he could no longer contain himself and began to run at great speed. He ran as fast as he could down the long, wide main street. He was going so fast that he began to attract the attention of others, and when they looked at him they laughed and said: "Ah, he's just the school fool" or "He's the sheep fool." Some of his siblings saw him and ran to tell their parents. They were very embarrassed and shouted at him: "Sebastian! Sebastian! Stop, stop! Stop running, you're a fool and you look ridiculous!"

But Sebastian didn't listen to anyone, he only felt his heart beating fast. The wind was crashing against his chest, and his hair was ruffled because of the speed. Although some of his brothers tried to stop him, they were unsuccessful. He did not stop until he reached the old man's house.

When he arrived, he was so tired that he just lay down on the ground and looked at the sky. He realized that the sunlight was almost gone, almost ready to give way to the darkness of night.

The old man was lighting a fire and some torches. Neither of them said anything to each other, but Sebastian began to cry and, as he looked at the sky of different colors caused by the setting sun, he still seemed to hear the voice of his brothers and his father shouting in front of everyone: "Sebastian, you are a fool! You are a wretch and you shame us!"

Sebastian closed his eyes tightly, letting out painful tears, and screamed as loud as he could. As he screamed, he remembered about the ring, how the jewelers begged him to sell it to them and that they would pay large sums of money for it while others had scorned it.

Filled with curiosity, he wiped away his tears, hurried to his feet, looked around for the old man, and saw that he was already sitting quietly by the fire. He held in his hand a vessel of a material like bronze. On the fire was a pot, as before, but this time it was made of clay. The old man reached out and plunged the bronze cup into the pot and took out a delicious hot tea then sweetened it with honey. He held out his hand offering the tea to Sebastian, who got closer and, taking the tea with his hand, sat down on the other side of the fire, which illuminated his face. The night was coming.

He took a sip of tea, looked at the old man, and in a very broken voice said:

"Kind sir, I am very confused. I think I understand everything and at the same time, I don't understand anything."

"Then let's start with parts," said the old man. "First tell me, what made you cry like that? Why did I see you arrive in despair and with so much anger?'

"Oh, yes, I'm sorry," Sebastian answered, somewhat embarrassed. "As usual, I was confused by some things I couldn't understand about the events of the ring, so I headed this way to ask you, but I started to feel something very strange and I couldn't resist the urge to run, and the truth is, I didn't even realize I was running until everyone looked at me. Among the people, my brothers appeared and made fun of me, as before, although I sensed that some of them were glad to see me again."

» "One of them went to tell my parents and they came to the street and began to shout at me as before. In everyone's ears, they shouted my name, and said I was a miserable fool, and could never do anything right. It reminded me that my whole life was always like that. I thought about stopping and pleading as before for them to understand me, that all I wanted was to love them and to be loved as I am, but looking at their faces full of anger and those of some of my brothers, full of some kind of envy, made me run more. As I ran, I felt that something was left behind, I don't know how to explain it.

» "I couldn't stop running because as I was running I felt lighter like something was coming off of me and that made me feel good."

» "Somehow I knew that my place is not with them, but I am more confused now because, before, I knew for sure that my life was over and now I don't know. I think that with that ring experience, life wants to teach me something but I don't know what it is and I'm sure you do. I beg you, wise old man, tell me what it is, why do I feel this?"

At that moment, Sebastian got up, sat down almost in front of him, put his hands on his arms, shook him a little, and said to him:

"I beg you to tell me what that was about the ring! Please! You knew that I would be offered a lot for it, that's why you told me not to sell it! Please explain, sir!"

The old man also took him by the arm.

"Calm down! Calm down! Dear Sebastian, life brought you here to show you what you have now realized."

"Explain to me better, please."

"Look, when you went to sell the ring to the common people, even though you begged them, they didn't want to buy it from you because they thought it was too high a price. They looked down on it because they didn't know about the piece of jewelry. This means that they had the opportunity to have a jewel in their hands that could have lifted them out of poverty, but they did not do it because they did not know the value it represents. Then you went back and showed it to the people who do know about jewelry, and they looked at the ring and quickly recognized its value and wanted to own it. They offered you a lot of money for it, didn't they?"

"Yes, sir. In fact, one offered me two hundred coins. And, as you say, he was a jewelry expert."

"Exactly. Now, do you understand, Sebastian? This ring is you, who has only been in the presence and hands of people who don't know your value because they don't know these things."

Sebastian took out the ring and took it in his hands. By then, the night was already very dense and the light of the campfire reflected on it.

"Am I like this ring?"

At that moment, his eyes opened wide and lit up.

"Of course! Of course! Now I understand. You mean that the people I've lived with don't know about jewels."

"That's right, my dear friend. You are a very valuable jewel, but you sought the approval of people who don't know what you are worth. That's why inside you lost your value, but now that you have understood that don't let others decide how much you are worth. Stay away from all those who take away value from your life."

> *You are a very valuable jewel, but you were seeking approval from people who don't know your worth.*

"But why do people who can love me look at me like a fool and want me to feel that way?"

"Well, do you remember how the jewelers were surprised when they saw the ring?"

"Yes, sir. In fact, the last jeweler put it with many others; that's where I could see a big difference. When I looked at the ring alone, I didn't see anything different, but when it was next to many others, it was very easy to understand that it was different. What I don't understand is, what makes it more valuable than the rest of the other rings of the same material? Even if they want to pay a lot, it is still just a ring."

"Actually, my dear Sebastian, jewelers weren't trying to buy the ring because of the material it's made of, but because of the creativity of its creator. Even you said

LIFE LEAKAGES

that only until you looked at it next to the other rings did you see the difference, and that's what makes it special. The jewelers knew that, by getting that ring, they could examine it and get ideas to make new designs. What I want you to learn is that when you are different, is really easy to be distinguished, and ignorant people will say that you are not worth it, but the ones who do notice the difference, will say that you are unique and authentic; that's what increases your value. In conclusion, you came here for some advice and it's an advice that I'll give you now:"

> *The problem you are a victim of is that you want the ignorant to know your value.*

» "The problem you are a victim of is that you want the ignorant to know your worth, but remember that you aren't worth according to what they know about you, but for what you are."

"So, forgive those who have slighted you. Think about the people who didn't want to pay even two coins for this ring, they didn't do it for lack of money, but because they were ignorant of the true value of the object that they had on their hands."

» "In the same way, the people who have hurt you didn't do it with the intention of hurting you, but because they didn't know they were hurting you. Therefore forgive them and ask for forgiveness, love them and let them love you, but when it comes to take decisions or moving forward with something important in your life, don't go with the ones who don't know and neither seek for their approval. Rather go with the experts, and they are the ones who will be able to see your value, they will tell you that you are capable and will give you good advice."

» "My friend, life has hit you and everything you have lived through hasn't been easy, but I want you to look at something."

The old man took the ring from him and threw it violently to the ground. Then he asked him:

"You see? Now it's full of dust. Do you think the jewelers will still see value in it?"

"Of course, sir, absolutely. The ring is dirty, but it still has the same value."

Then the old man stood on top of the ring, began to stomp on it, and said:

"Do you see now, Sebastian? Besides, I think it's not worth anything and that it's trash."

At that moment, tears began to roll down Sebastian's cheeks. He had already understood that this ring represented his life and that many people had tramped on it in some way.

"What are you thinking, Sebastian?" Asked the old man while he kept stomping on it. "Now it's been stepped on, and it's full of dust, and I've said that it isn't worth anything and that it's trash." Finally, the old man stopped and said: "Now I ask you: Do you think that the jewelers will keep offering you the same amount for it?"

"Yes, sir, I'm sure of that."

"Good."

The old man picked up the ring and threw it to the barnyard, where there were some pigs. The jewel, quickly, began to sink in the mud and manure.

"Good thing that you learned the lesson with the ring! But now it's not worth anything because I, who is known as a sage, have thrown it to the mud and manure. It's not worth taking it out of there because, at last, no one will give anything for it. Don't you think?"

LIFE LEAKAGES

"Of course not, that ring can't stay in that place because I'm sure that it still has the same value. If I take it right now with a jeweler, they'll be happy to buy it. Let's get it out of there, please."

"We will, my dear friend, only because you are right. The ring is still very valuable for it to stay in the mud and manure. But I'll only get it out when you promise me that you won't stay in the mud and manure where people dumped you after stepping on you and hurting you, because that's what made you think you were worthless. If you have understood that, just like the ring, that doesn't diminish your value, then you are allowed to take that jewel out of that mud and manure, but you must know that if you get it out of there, you will also be getting out your soul and you will never again allow anyone to dump you in that place again."

"I understand, and I also understand that I'm the one responsible for my life and that's why, today, I decide to live. I never imagined that all my life would change only in one day. I thank the heavens that I found you and that you didn't give up on me. You taught me that I'm worth a lot and that I deserve to live, so today I'll take responsibility for my life, I will live and let others live.

I understand that I am responsible for my life and that is why today I decide to live.

LIFE LEAKAGES

Chapter 16
DON'T LET THE OUTSIDE COME INSIDE YOU

And just as it happened to our friend Sebastian, it can also be that around you there are people who are causing you low self-esteem. Because not only marriage can be toxic, but all those relationships with people who, with or without your permission, influence your life.

It is said that we define ourselves by the first seven people we spend the most time with. This means that depending on how those closest to you are, so will you be.

I believe that the deepest wounds in a human being are almost always formed within a home. It is always the family that gets hurt the most because when you feel love for someone you become very vulnerable and very prone to being hurt.

Remember that God gave you potential and talent that others do not have; therefore, others will not understand you when you tell them about your ideas and plans. In fact, many times they will even try to encourage you to abandon those dreams and goals that were born in your heart at some point. The problem begins when you decide to listen to them, so they won't be angry with you. Then you abandon your dreams, your plans, and your ideas, and when you do this a part of you begins to die inside. You begin to think and pretend to be someone you are not. You feel empty because you are no longer living as you, but the life of one of your family.

> *God gave you potential and talent that others do not have; therefore, others will not understand you.*

It may be the person who influences you the most, perhaps your father, your mother, some other relative, or simply a friend you love and appreciate. Then you start a war of survival because you gave up your life to please another person.

That is the reason why many people do not find meaning in their lives: At some point, they gave up their own lives and began to do what others told them was best. As human beings, we want to seek approval, we want others, or at least the people we love, to be proud of us, and so we do everything to achieve this. Thus, renouncing ourselves and we start living according to other people's perspectives.

But today, I want to encourage you to be aware that you are still alive. And as they say: 'while there is life, there is hope.' I encourage you to live your life, and forget what others may think of you because people who do not live their lives will not want you to live yours either.

Remember that it is very different to live than to exist. Today, we can see many cars running at high speed on the roads but these cars have no life, they just exist. Today, it is very common to see airplanes flying in the sky, and we are even impressed by them, but they just exist, they have no life. In the same way, we can make a long list of things that only exist, but they do not live because it is someone else who is driving their engines. There are thousands of people who think they are living because they move and breathe but in reality, they are not living. Everything they do is because someone else is driving them. But I am writing this for you today so that this doesn't happen to you.

LIFE LEAKAGES

I have heard so many parents say that everything they do is for their children. This is terrible because, although it sounds very nice, if we put this phrase in the light of life we realize that these parents stopped living because they became slaves of their children's lives and no longer live to fulfill their purpose in this life.

Today, we see so many people tied to a terrible marriages. They suffer physical and verbal abuse, and when you ask them why they put up with such a terrible life and do nothing to get out of that relationship, you will hear the famous phrase: "I do it and endure all this for my children."

Do you see? These are people who are no longer living, but are only existing to serve their children or spouse. On certain occasions, I have had to officiate the ceremony of a funeral. I like to arrive early because it allows me time to talk with the relatives of the recently deceased. When they tell me how their life was, most of the time I realize that the person had already been dead for years and that what we are really doing in that place is a ceremony for the end of their existence.

So I encourage you to not only exist but to live because a living person can do so much more for the people they love. Live and teach others to live. Start doing that thing you dreamed one day you would do. Set yourself a dream or some goal and work hard to achieve it or set yourself a dream so big that it even scares you and challenges you. When you feel the challenges of the risks and the adrenaline that comes from making decisions, you will realize that you are alive because that is what life is all about: deciding to *live* or just to *exist*.

FINAL ACKNOWLEDGMENTS

Writing this book was more than a wonderful experience. It was like an adventure where I had the joy of working as a team with extraordinary people. It was during this process where I met Karla (Gabi Gutierrez) whom I thank for all her support and her great participation in a professional way. She was the one who supported me during the entire publishing process: from organizing the ideas for the creation of the first draft of the book, the writing, and proofreading, guiding me through the design, the editorial process, to the final publication of the physical and digital versions of the work. Not only did she help me with the writing, but a mentor from whom I received a lot of guidance and direction, which was very essential to be able to finish my book.

I also thank Yolanda Chapa and Aurora Carranza for editing this book and transforming my humble words into something professional, making it possible to read simply and understandably everything that had been written.

To Andrea Saga, who transformed my imagination into something palpable and managed to design a cover image with a lot of styles and a lot of resemblance to what I had in my mind. And although it was a long process, they never gave up. I believe that not only did we manage to create a book but we also managed to learn how to persevere and conquer what at first seemed to be impossible and to give shape to what is still in the mind of an individual. For everything, thank you very much.

www.ingramcontent.com/pod-product-compliance
Lightning Source LLC
Chambersburg PA
CBHW032122090426

42743CB00007B/426